GOIN' HOME

Other books by Timeri Murari

Novels

THE MARRIAGE
THE OBLIVION TAPES
LOVERS ARE NOT PEOPLE
THE LAST RUN

Non-fiction

THE NEW SAVAGES
INDIA—THE EVIL WITHIN (editor)

Plays

GRENADE
LOVERS ARE NOT PEOPLE

Television
ONLY AN AMERICA (series)

GOIN' HOME

by

Timeri Murari

G. P. Putnam's Sons
New York

103889

With grateful thanks to Thames Television, London, for giving permission to quote from interviews in their film documentary. And to Alexandra Sumner for her excellent research.

Library of Congress Cataloging in Publication Data

Murari, Timeri.
  Goin' home.

  1. Afro-American families. 2. Stanford family.
3. Rural-urban migration—United States. I. Title.
E185.86.M95 1980   973'.04'96073   79-13666
ISBN 0-399-12384-9

For my
dear friends
Michael & Judith

GOIN' HOME

CHAPTER 1

The City Folk

The car is very special. It is a maroon, two door, white topped, glittering '74 Buick. On the front number plate is the flowing legend "Slick Daddy Kool," and a decal sticker on the rear side window warns the envious: "If you value your life as much as I value this car, don't fuck with it." The interior is equally flamboyant. A couple of foam dice hang from the rear view window, the front seats are covered with imitation sheepskin, and set in the dash is an 8-track stereo system and a CB radio. The aerial for this is a ten foot high polished steel whip set on the rear bumper. On the driver's door is neatly printed "Arthur." On the passenger's side "Alma." The lettering is an inch high.

A frequent sight on Evelyn street, in Mattapan, Boston, is Arthur Dean Stanford cleaning and polishing this car. He fulfills this labor of love three, possibly four, times a week, depending on how the weather has soiled his car and the judgment of his own critical eye. He has even done this job, to the surprise of his neighbors who are used to this eccentricity, standing hip deep in fresh snow.

Arthur is a slight small man. He isn't more than five foot eight and wears his hair in a medium length Afro, which adds an inch or two to his height, if not to his breadth. He is a pale brown and his face is delicate. He has a fine slim nose, high cheekbones, serious brown eyes and a sensual mouth. He always dresses in a smart, casual style—safari suits or leather jackets—except when cleaning his car, then it's old jeans and work boots. But once he's finished he changes quickly, as if not wanting to be seen in shabby clothes. There is a certain vanity in Arthur. Although he needs to wear glasses constantly, he only does so when he's behind the wheel of his car. They are expensive glasses with 14-carat gold frames.

He is also a shy, introverted man. When he first meets strangers, he is given to long silences. This, with his general quietness, gives me the impression that he could also be easily bullied. Silences can be thoughtful or empty, and I'm not sure, when we first meet, which category his fall into.

"This neighborhood didn't use to be this . . . this way," Arthur Dean says. He speaks slowly and with a stammer. He has a tendency to split his words, emphasizing the first syllable and then letting the rest fade away. "When the blacks began moving in then the whites, they move out gradually you know, and now it become mostly blacks living on this street. Then the Asians begin movin' in and the blacks are moving' out so I guess it's just somethin' gonna be, you know.

Evelyn Street is about half a mile long and one way. The houses on either side, built in the 1930s and '40s are all three- or four-story wood-framed. They have shingle roofs and wood porches and each of the apartments above ground level has a wooden balcony. There is a two- to three-square-yard "lawn" in front of each house, and behind a fairly large yard. It is a tree-lined street. All the houses on Evelyn Street could do with a coat of fresh paint, and many of the porches need a few more planks of wood, and possibly more nails and struts to keep them from sagging. Some look like wooden hammocks, and the balconies on the second and third floors slope dangerously. The house on the corner, fifty yards down from Arthur Dean, has been gutted by fire. Its skeleton looks forlorn in the afternoon sunlight. There are two or three abandoned cars parked on streets. Their tires are flat, their windows broken, their interiors gutted and torn.

"The last white family used to live in that corner house," Arthur says. "They were nice people," he adds wistfully. "I don't know why they moved. This was a few months after we came here. Summer of '76."

It isn't, as yet, too difficult to imagine what Evelyn Street must have looked like. The houses must have shone with fresh paint, the porches must have stood upright and needed little repair, and those sloping balconies must have jutted as straight as a prow. Mostly white middle-class families lived on this street. There couldn't have been a black face to be seen, except for a delivery boy, and those white children must have played on the street and in their yards like these new black tenants do.

The changes in the neighborhood began to occur in the late '60s. Prior to that there weren't that many black people in Boston. They only constituted five percent of the city's population, although Boston had a long and honorable tradition of tolerance toward black people. It was in this city, in 1863, that Lincoln's Emancipation Proclamation was read from the balcony of the Tremont Temple. It is one of the sights to be visited in Boston, and there is a large metal plaque on the side of the building to constantly remind visitors of its past.

In spite of its liberal tradition, few blacks from the South made the journey to Boston. The roads that headed North led to the industrial cities of Detroit and Chicago and Philadelphia and New York. The migration pattern over the century lay in straight South–North lines, and Boston, a city of learning and culture, had little employment to offer black people.

In the 1950s, Boston, in keeping with its history, welcomed the first freedom riders with pomp and civic ceremony and stirring speeches. Heartened by the welcome, more blacks began to migrate from the South into the city. In the '60s, their numbers swelled to nine percent of the population. In 1979, the black population has risen to twenty percent of the total and Boston looks on its minority with cold, unfriendly eyes.

By the time Arthur Dean Stanford moved into his neighborhood, Evelyn Street was ninety-nine percent black. Mattapan, like Roxbury and North Dorchester, had become an involuntarily segregated black neighborhood.

I had met Arthur and his wife Alma once before. It was a chance meeting—a friend mentioned to a friend that they knew the Stanford family. For me, they were unique. I had been searching for them for months, not specifically Arthur and Alma, but a black family that was going to return to a home in the South permanently. A year earlier, in 1978, the United States Census Bureau had reported that for the first time in the history of the country a remigration was taking place. Blacks were moving back South in appreciable numbers. I was curious to know why there was this new permutation of the search for the American Dream.

Perhaps the movement is not really so new. In October, 1946, W. E. B. DuBois gave a moving speech in South Carolina to the Southern Youth Legislature which seems to anticipate the results of the census:

> The future of the American Negro is in the South. Here three hundred and twenty-seven years ago, they began to enter what is now the United States of America; here they have made their greatest contribution to American culture;

12

and here they have suffered the damnation of slavery, the frustration of reconstruction and the lynching of emancipation. Here is the magnificent climate; here is the fruitful earth under the beauty of the Southern sun; and here, if anywhere on earth, is the need of the thinker, the worker and the dreamer. . . . There are enormous opportunities here for a new nation, a new economy, a new culture in a South really new and not a mere renewal of an old South of Slavery, monopoly and race hate.

Arthur, though he'd never read DuBois, had heard the South, his South, was changing. He'd read a few newspaper stories, but mostly the word traveled through his friends and relatives. There were good jobs in the South; there was more industry, and, most important, there was a new era of tolerance.

"It is partly that," Arthur says, "but it's also my own opinion that I think it's better in the South. Like here you make money and the cost of livin' is so high. You make it and spend it right back out. There you don't make as much but it don't cost you as much to live and you can live more comfortably. And they don't have such bad winters down there."

Arthur had made the decision to move South, back to his home in Alabama, after the winter of 1978. It had been a long cold winter and the blizzards had been fierce. He'd lived in Boston seven years, and each winter had worn him down a little bit more. Arthur and Alma consented to allow me to accompany them back South. I wasn't sure how Arthur viewed me. In the beginning, we had difficulty just understanding each other's accent, his Alabaman, mine British. He accepted my presence and interest equally. I was for him an outsider, an Indian with a British background. I also came with a curiosity about the South. The South is the new world I had never explored. I had read about it extensively. Black and white

13

writers, fiction, nonfiction, newspaper stories. But it is difficult to experience this world from the words of other men. The writings of the black men and women have been bitter, hurt, angry, while the whites write about a different and convoluted world. It is strange. Neither group of authors people their books, except on the periphery, with members of the other race.

My curiosity is not to be one-sided. I need to try to understand Arthur and the white people he grew up with in the South and I know there will be times I will not succeed. The world I am about to enter is theirs as much as his and I am inquisitive to know as much about it as I will be allowed.

Arthur isn't a highly educated man. He finished high school in Baker Hill, Alabama, and almost immediately left home for Boston.

"Well, the reason I come here I was just out of school and it was a free trip," Arthur says. "I didn't have much money and my brother was here too, and he wanted me to come to Boston so I came and I've been here ever since." Boston could well have been Los Angeles or Detroit. It isn't the city that attracted him, but his brother's presence. "He never talked too much about Boston, you know. But I had pictures in my mind. I thought it was goin' to be like those pictures on television, you know. When I got here, I was really amazed it was so much different. I figured Boston would be nice and clean and big wide streets. Nice and peaceful. It's so much different. Trash all over the place, streets all torn up and stuff, you know."

He gives a final flick of the polishing rag over the chrome of his car. It shines, as if new, in the fall sun. "You know," he says softly, "I'm goin' to keep this car till it falls apart. I ain't cared for a car like this ever." Arthur has had many cars. Cars are his passion. He learned to drive when he was six, while sitting on the lap of his father. He put together his own car, from bits and pieces in the scrapyards, when he was fourteen. There appears to be little he doesn't know about a car. At the moment, he has a job spray-painting cars, and when his car was bumped by a police car and the wing dented, he touched up the damage himself.

"They never gave me compensation," he says as we turn away from the car and go into the apartment house. "I applied but . . . ." He shrugs.

His apartment house is well shaded by trees. There should be a rocker on this worn wooden porch with its sagging railings, but there isn't. The front door is open. The stairs leading up his third-floor apartment are narrow and sharply angular. There is comfortable space for only one person to climb at a time, carefully. On the corners, the steps are narrow.

Arthur Dean's front balcony, which is only two steps from his front door, is cluttered with his discarded possessions. Like the others on the street, it slopes down. Against the front rails, contributing to the frailty of the structure is a set of weights. He bought them on a whim to build up his physique. Now they are discolored from lack of use. There are also a couple of broken chairs and a mattress.

Arthur Dean's two-bedroom apartment is what the real estate brokers call a "floor-through." The front door opens onto a hall which passes a bedroom to the right, a large living room to the left, and a kitchen at the end and then out onto the back porch.

The living room is divided in two. One half is dominated by a huge Philco color television set. It runs constantly even if no one is watching it. The couches are black imitation leather and they squeak whenever someone sits on them. The other part of the living room has its own centerpiece—an expensive Morse Dictagraph sound system. This too runs all the time. The music is invariably by black artists. The one tape that is played over and over again is by the Staple Singers, and their favorite song is "Unlock Your Mind." Leading off the front room is the master bedroom. The window overlooks some trees in the backyard. Centered in the bedroom is a massive waterbed. It takes up nearly two-thirds of the space.

The kitchen is spacious. It has a small, circular dining table, with straight-backed chairs to one side, and there is more than enough room left over to move around easily.

Alma is trying to sort out what she is going to take on their move, and what to leave behind. The contrast between Arthur and Alma is striking. She is more confident, more extroverted. A slim striking woman, her face is heart-shaped with a strong jaw, prominent cheekbones, a pretty nose and an expressive mouth. She has a gold tooth: it is a broad shining incisor. It has been a long time since I've seen such a gold tooth. It belongs to another era when only the rich wore gold in their mouths.

Alma is twenty-four and has an engaging quality composed of both boldness and shyness. The shyness appears affected at times. When she's spoken to, she bends her head away and down, as if she doesn't want to face the person addressing her. Then she peeps up, studies the person seriously, and laughs before replying. From our earliest meeting she is much easier to talk to; though the blend of coqeutry and outspokenness keeps me off balance. I am never sure whether she is amused or impatient with my questions. I imagine courting her must have been difficult. It took Arthur six months and only his patience could finally have interpreted the dips and turns of her moods.

She speaks differently from Arthur. Hers is a Northern accent. The words are quick, clipped, yet she too comes from the South. Her parents live in Memphis, Tennessee, and she too, like Arthur, left home and went North the moment she was of age.

"I had a sister here," Alma says, "so that's why I picked Boston." Her voice lilts. It drops and rises an octave. She is more nervous than she reveals and laughs between sentences. "All I wanted to do was just get away from the South. I didn't hear nothing about Boston. All I know is a city in the North, so I just came."

Alma came to Boston in 1972. Unlike Arthur she was aware that if she was to do well she needed something more than a high school diploma. She enrolled at the ITT technical school, and took a course as a nurse's aide.

"Another reason I come here," Alma says as we move into the living room, "was because I got tired with down South. The only thing I could find as work was like farming, picking cotton, gardening, picking beans and stuff like that to make a living. I graduated from high school in 1971, and the only job there was picking cotton, and you could make like three dollars a hundred, so to make any money I had to pick . . . I mean make *any* money . . . least pick three hundred a day which was only nine dollars still. So if like that was the only job you had for the week, you would bring home like thirty dollars or twenty-five dollars. Depends on how much cotton you pick. I used to pick two hundred and fifty and pull a nine-foot sack all day on my back."

"What is a 'hundred'?"

"Pounds," Alma says and laughs. "Don't you know anything? I was paid three dollars to pick one hundred pounds of cotton. I did it from six o'clock to six o'clock, with a nine-foot sack on my back."

As she is only five foot four and a half, I can't visualize how she did it.

"It's over your shoulder," Alma says, "and . . . you drag it on the ground behind you."

"You drag it," Arthur says. "I sure never did that. I have picked cotton, but nothin' like the way Alma picked. I never picked seven hundred pounds that whole week you know, and so I never did too well."

The apartment, with its expensive gadgets, glass-topped tables, mirrors framed in gold-colored sun rays,

17

vinyl sofas, and vibrating armchairs, is an antithesis to their past poverty. There isn't any part of their past in the apartment.

Visually, it has been erased from their lives. They have overcome the failure of their birthright, and though the past still exists in their memories, and is immediate in their telling, it is receding further and further behind them. At this moment I am unaware, apart from the mention of manual struggle, of what it is like to be a black in the South. All I see in these first few days, is a moderately successful young family.

Tavis's presence is highly visible in the apartment, even when he isn't. The bedroom off the front hall is scattered with his toys. It is furnished with an adult's bed, rather than a child's. His sturdy tricycle remains parked in the hall, and his books lie in the front room. When Arthur and Alma are both working, Tavis spends most of his time with Alma's sister. When I do meet him, there is no mistaking the resemblance between Arthur and his son. They both have the same features. It is a graceful face, fashioned delicately of lightly browned skin, almost European in its impression. Tavis is three and just about reaches my knees. He is at the stage when he makes a lot of noise. When he was born, Arthur wanted to call him Thomas; Alma wanted Davis. The compromise was Tavis. His middle name, LeShaun, was Alma's invention, and Arthur only discovered that when he read the birth certificate. Tavis, in spite of being the only child, isn't spoiled. Both of them keep him firmly in line, although they will often succumb with the natural indulgence of young parents.

"I would like Tavis to have his ground roots back in the South," Arthur Dean says. "This is really his home, but that's more of a home than this." He stops, trying to articulate the confusion he feels between his own present, and his past. "How do I want to say this? He was born here, and this is really his home, but . . . my home is back

18

there and . . ." He halts, gives up. "I think it'll be better, you know, for him."

Alma tilts her head, and looks at Arthur. She looks skeptical. She closes her eyes, and tosses her head, as if dismissing Arthur's reasoning.

"I think it could be good for Tavis," she says, though she doesn't sound as if she's totally convinced. She has, though she doesn't articulate it now, a distaste for the South. She reveals the exasperation, a certain resignation, in her face which sometimes runs in conflict with what she is saying. "But when Tavis grows up, I want him to make up his own mind, whether he wants to stay there or come back to the North. Whichever he decides, it's up to him. But as far as going to college when he gets old enough to go to college, I would rather for him to go to college here. Because I know Boston has the best schools and the most schools in the United States.

In spite of this hesitation on her part, of the two, Alma appears the more confident that she and Arthur will be successful down South.

CHAPTER 2

Boston

Boston and its environs, from the air, resembles a European city. Apart from downtown Boston, with its tall commercial buildings, it spreads generously, with the river winding through down to the bay, instead of springing abruptly, like a Manhattan or a Chicago, into the air. On a crisp fall day, you can catch the countless complex details. Out in the bay, with the sun glittering on the water, you can see the sailboats tacking back and forth across the bay; in the downtown area the blend of malls and high-rises and old granite historical buildings; in Beacon Hill the London-like railed-in garden surrounded by expensive townhouses; the almost Dickensian narrowness of some of the Beacon Hill streets; and from there it spreads out into its suburbs of Cambridge and Mattapan and South Boston and Dorchester.

Harvard Yard is only a few miles from Evelyn Street. It is another world; enclosed by high brick walls and wrought iron gates. The yard is crisp underfoot with fallen leaves, and the sun filters down on the heads of the young students through the thinning branches. I had forgotten how quiet and calm an academic world is, and how innocent youth can look. They are, to paraphrase, the best and the brightest. Nearly all are white; here and there, because of their rarity, a black face is instantly visible. Few here will labor. The richest prizes of the American Dream will be theirs for the taking. Not one of them will ever know what it's like to pick and chop cotton twelve hours a day for three dollars a hundred.

There are so many great educational institutions in and around the Boston area. MIT, Boston University, Yale, Brandeis. One would suspect that all this intelligence and talent would have some influence on the politics of the city, but the universities seem to have little interest in or effect on Boston's politics.

The greater Boston area is composed of a complex of zones. If one, though scattered, is academic, another is white Irish. South Boston has some resemblance to both Mattapan and Harvard Yard. Like Mattapan, the shop windows are also covered with wire mesh, abandoned cars squat on worn tires in the streets, and there are gaps of vacant and rubble-strewn land. There seem to be innumerable little Catholic churches which are never too far from a saloon. South Boston has the same feel as Mattapan. A sense of harsh struggle and hard lives and an approaching desolation. There is a strong sense of community, and continuity. The Irish, who at the beginning of this century were the social outcasts of Boston politics and social life, have now gained political power. South Boston's representatives control City Hall, and its men man the city police. (I am told St. Patrick's Day in Boston makes the New York celebrations insignificant.) Its resemblance to Harvard Yard is more subtle. There are no black faces to be seen on these South Boston streets. If in Harvard Yard the barrier is wealth, here it is fear. "You can get yourself killed walkin' into South Boston," I am told by many black people.

21

This antagonism and competition between white and black has become more visible over the last few years. Some of the worst busing riots in the country have occurred in Boston. As a result of this, the sense of greater Boston as an area of clearly demarcated war zones becomes apparent.

"Probably to start off with I'd have to send Tavis to a nursery school, and those are segregated in Boston," Alma says. "Then he would have to be bused, like to probably Forest High Park."

"I would prefer him to go to a desegregated school," Arthur says. "It's better all the way around, because how else can you make it? You gotta live together when you get grown, and, you know, compete for the same things so why not go to the same school and get the same education you know. Give each child the same opportunity. Right?"

As we look out of the window down at Evelyn Street while we talk, we watch two black boys riding up and down on scooters. They accelerate past, slow, skid-turn, accelerate back. Further up the street, three or four black women stand talking.

"This was a nice area when we first came here," Alma says almost defensively. "It was quiet, clean and everything. It was kids on the streets, but it wasn't like it is now. Kids out at all hours of the night, and stuff like that. It wasn't Asians on the streets, and now Puerto Ricans have moved in. And there are no whites left. Kids have also started stealing cars and leaving them here, so the street has really gone down during the time we've been here."

The idea that others are to blame for the decline in her street is depressing to Alma. She remains at the window a moment longer; disapprovingly eyeing the boys still riding back and forth.

"When I first came to Boston I liked it here," she continues. "Because like the jobs I've had—I've worked a million places since I've been here—at that first job it made me feel better because the whites actually got along better with the blacks here than they do down South. Down South you really feel bad when you go and try and get a job with a white. They look at you like you're crazy, like you . . . you are out of your place, you know. You're not supposed to be there. But here it wasn't like that and I was surprised to see how well that some blacks and whites got along. Myself, I get along with anybody if they give me a chance."

Yet she remains wistful. It's as if what she has just said, she doesn't truly believe. That first euphoria has long since worn off, and in its place is a deep sense of loss.

"Sure I had a white friend," Alma begins fiercely, then falters. "But somehow I don't know what happened. She stopped calling. It's just like . . . I don't know what happened. We would . . . she'd come over and stay all night and we would go out together, then all of a sudden she just stopped. I don't know why. We used to work together. I don't know what happened."

Arthur starts to say something, but only clears his throat. Alma broods in the silence. Since that one failure, Alma hasn't made an effort to become friendly with other white people. Her closest friend in Boston is a black woman from the Caribbean island Dominica.

"I don't distrust white people," Alma says. "I trust them to a degree, just as they trust us to a degree. To a point."

She fidgets, wanting to say more. I can understand her difficulty over that relationship. One cannot help but confuse race with personality. Did the relationship break over a simple personal dislike; or were their racial reasons? It is so easy to substitute one for another, and to disentangle them needs a discerning eye, for who wants to believe that one can be personally disliked. (A white person is lucky. He never has that problem.)

"I don't know why, but somehow white people think

they are superior to the black people," Alma says. "They think they are far much better than we are. Even the poor white people look down on black people."

Tavis, who returned earlier from his sitter's, is in his room. He has kept himself occupied playing and talking to himself. Often, when he recognizes a particular tune on the stereo, he will "sing" a few bars over and over again. He emerges from his room, wearing jeans and a sweat shirt, and goes to look out of the window, before coming to hug Alma. She expertly plaits his hair and asks: "What do you want?"

"Out," he says and points.

Alma goes to get herself ready to take him to the playlot, and Tavis moves over to hug Arthur. He treats them equally in his affections, confident in both. However, the final arbitrator in any disagreements between Alma and Tavis is settled by Arthur.

The sandlot is not on Evelyn Street, but a block and a half away across Norfolk Street. It is a main road, with fast two-way traffic. Alma is frightened of allowing Tavis to play down on Evelyn Street and each day takes him across to the sandlot for an hour or more.

Today, Arthur decides to come along as well, though they do take turns with Tavis. They are a handsome couple, with Tavis between them, Alma in a loose shirt and jeans and Arthur wearing a leather jacket and slacks.

Arthur ambles; Alma hurries, and is always a step or two ahead. Tavis is pulled slightly askew, but he is obviously used to this family trait.

Arthur met Alma in Boston when they were both working temporarily for Polaroid. He courted her for six months, and then they were married on July 20, 1974, in Alma's church in Tipton County, Tennessee. She'd wanted to be married in the South with her family around her. There is a wedding photograph of them in the front room. It's in color and silver framed. Arthur, looking so young, almost a boy, is dressed in a powder-blue tuxedo with a ruffled shirt; Alma wears a white bridal dress. On either side of them are their respective mothers. All the faces in the photograph reflect a quiet dignity, and pride in the celebration.

"I've never put down roots in Boston," Arthur says as we stop for the traffic. A hot dog van pulls up on our side of the road, and children from the sandlot opposite duck and weave through the traffic to get to the van. "I always felt Boston was just a little stoppin'-off place."

"Sure, I agree with Arthur," Alma says as we start to cross. "Boston was like an opportunity to further my eduation, to come here and go to school, but I really never accepted it as being my home. I always said my home is down South." She leans down and kisses Tavis. "Isn't it, Tavis? He's a Bostonian so when he goes down there he's gonna be a Northerner and I'll be a Southerner. I think it'll be better for him 'cause down there he has a chance to get out. He don't have to be cooped up in one place all the time. He can go outside and I won't have to worry about something happening to him or somebody coming down the street driving like crazy and running over him or something like that. It'll be better for him."

Alma takes Tavis into the fenced-in sandlot. There are perhaps forty or fifty other children playing on the swings and the slides and the climbing rungs. A solitary mongrel plays tag with three children. Tavis, under the watchful eye of Alma, runs back and forth crazily, as if trying to release all his energy in one burst.

Arthur remains slightly aloof, watching a few older kids playing basketball on a court next to the sandlot. One, tall and lithe, is especially good.

"I never had much time to play games," he says. "Never did in school, and here I work a lot of overtime." He is proud of his skilled hands and his ability to support his family so well. "When I first came to Boston I lived in Cambridge. The only job that there have been any racial problems, you know, like make me feel I'm looked down on because I'm black, is the job that I'm on now as a spray painter."

Like Alma, Arthur has had many jobs during his stay in Boston. He first worked for Mastercall, quit a couple of times and returned to them, until they went out of business. Then he'd worked with his brother Heywood in an electronics firm for a while. Heywood had quit to become a riot cop, and Arthur had wanted to follow, but, even though his application is still in, he has yet to be called for an interview. However, he's never had problems finding any of these jobs. He held a job as a stock clerk for a couple of years, then quit that and took the whole summer off.

"Then I worked in Polaroid for close to a year, where I met Alma," he says. "I quit there and moved South for a month or two. I come back here and found the job where I'm working at now."

The South, over a thousand miles away, haunts them both. It feels, from this distance as they talk about it, a mythical place; its hold on them is almost a physical force that's pulling them back. The hook is more in their hearts than in their minds. And they are in opposition. The heart says "go"; the mind "stay." Alma's unease has, over the days, increased. She's steeling herself for the return South like a superstitious person about to enter a graveyard long past the midnight hour.

If there is comfort in statistics and the game of numbers, then Arthur and Alma have little to fear. Forty black people a day migrate from the North into Atlanta alone. These numbers represent not only the skilled middle class moving to well-paid jobs with the growing industries in the South, but also the poor black. Over the last five years, over 2½ million people, both black and white have migrated South.

Arthur has no job to go to. He spent a week, earlier in the summer of '78, looking around Eufaula, Alabama. His family lives exactly nine miles away, outside the town of Baker Hill.

"When I go back, I'll be lookin' for work," he says. "I'm plannin' on goin' down to Techtronics, you know, to be interviewed for a job." Techtronics is a small firm in Eufaula. It makes electronic depth gauges. Arthur gives the impression they are only too eager to hire his services. "Sure, they told me I could start any time. Well . . . if that don't work, I'm goin' to try to collect unemployment until I find me a pretty decent job. I have a friend who's workin' for the Alabama gas company. They're a pretty good company to work for you know, they pay good money. He told me when I was home, he would take me down to where he worked at and talk to The Man about givin' me a job. Other friends have said the same thing."

He shows none of Alma's uneasiness. He is going home, his own home, and he expects to be at peace. His parents have also dangled a prize in front of him. His father owns more than a hundred acres of land in and around Baker Hill! He mentions this only in passing, and it comes as a surprise to me. A hundred acres, from this distance, seems a reasonable amount of property, and I now imagine his family to be more well off than I'd first thought.

"My great-grandfather bought the land," Arthur Dean says. "It's been in the family for well over a hundred years. He walked all the way to Montgomery with his savings, and paid cash for it. It cost . . . you know . . . a few cents an acre."

"This must have been just after Emancipation. How did he get the money?"

"He saved," Arthur says laconically. "I don' know how. You got to ask my father that." He watches his son a moment. Tavis is playing on the slide, and so is the mongrel dog. "When we go back, he promised to give us about ten acres to build our own house on," Arthur says.

"Sure we have a design for it. It's kind of a ranch house. Alma chose it. We got the drawin's all ready too. When I was back home in the summer I saw The Man in the bank. He said he'd give us a loan for the building."

When we return to the apartment, they bring out the blueprint. It is an architect's scale drawing of a ranch house with three bedrooms, a living room, a den, a large kitchen, garage. Alma had seen it in a magazine.

"Sure we're going to build it," Alma says. That long steady glance out of the corner of her eyes, and the sudden laugh. "We'll have our own home in no time. The rent and stuff that we pay here will be our own. Then we're going to try and rent out some of the other land, you know for things like growing food and a trailer park. We're going to do a lot with that land. Now it's just sitting there."

From this distance, everything they say appears feasible and easy, and these two are enthusiastic; they bloom with ideas and plans and dreams. That land is precious; it is the heart of Arthur's family, and they must have clung fiercely to every grain of earth and tree and root and rock to have been able to keep possession these hundred years.

"They have tried to take it away from us," Arthur says.

"Who's 'they'?"

"White people. They try to cheat us out of it, or they want to buy it away for nothin'. We won't let them." He sits back in the deep sofa, playing with his car keys, looking satisfied. "It'll be good to go back. I have my family there and they'll help and push me on you know. I can also grow some of the food we eat you know. Save money instead of buyin' at the store."

Alma gives Arthur one of her long, doubting glances and turns her head away. Her memory doesn't appear to be as idyllic as his; hers is of twelve-hour days in the cotton fields and the heat on her back. Alma doesn't talk much about her parents or her family in Tennessee. She keeps them vague and it takes some time to discover more about them.

From a distance the past can be enchanting. Our memories are unfailingly gentle when it deals with the events of our childhood and youth. That is a time of permanent summer in which sadness and pain and failure have been banished.

For Arthur the nostalgia is more acute. He remembers so clearly not only the past, but also the present of his land and his parents. The two are intertwined, his love for them and the land. He has a sense of identification with that piece of earth; he belongs to that place of his birth and eventual burial. He wants to be a part of the continuity of his family, for he also imagines the future for himself and his child. Most of us are not that fortunate. We have traveled and remained far from the place of our parents and our grandparents and great-grandparents. To some it's a place of mystery, long forgotten, long abandoned, and any return would be impossible. For Arthur the past is still within his grasp.

CHAPTER 3

The Parting

Friends and brothers and sisters and innumerable children, helping and hindering, clutter the apartment on the day of departure. Most of them belong to Alma. Willie ("Bear"), her oldest brother, a big, wide man who looks immensely strong, sits at the kitchen table with Paul, a family friend, sipping a beer. There is little family resemblance between the Bear and Alma. Bear came to Boston long before Alma. In Tennessee, he'd worked for a white man who'd run an illicit distillery making moonshine liquor. The police raided it one day and the only man to be jailed was the Bear. He got six months and the moment he was released he took off for Boston.

Alma's sister, Magreta ("Doc"), is helping Alma pack and to cater to the needs of all her guests. Doc does resemble the Bear. She isn't as large or as heavy, but her face is as square, compared to Alma's oval. Doc has brought her four children along, and they are playing with Tavis and getting in the way of the adult company. Doc is divorced and struggling to live on her welfare.

Mona, the woman from Dominica, is Alma's best friend. She has brought her two children along as well, and in between picking up things she and Alma chatter away.

Little has been done, although the Allied Van Lines truck is due this afternoon. Saturday, September 30 is a fine sunny day, and if it weren't for the packing cases in the middle of the living room, this could be a pleasant party. The stereo music can be heard from every room, children keep dashing in and out of the apartment, and the adults sit around and talk. Alma is desultorily throwing out all those unnecessary little things that somehow accumulate, like barnacles to the bottom of a ship, in one's life. Broken toys, cracked glasses, matchbooks of places they'd visited. Her mood seesaws. One moment she's excited; the next thoughtful and withdrawn.

Arthur is in the living room packing one of the crates with Tavis's toys. He does this carefully and thoughtfully. His mood is much lighter than Alma's. Heywood, his brother, sits near him. He looks very much like Arthur, except he is a few years older. He also stands and behaves like Arthur; full of quiet and laconic replies.

"You going to miss me?" Alma asks Bear and Doc.

"Sure," they both say and laugh. "Who's goin' to do our taxes and stuff like that? You looked after us real good Li'l Mama."

"You'll have to send your papers down to Eufaula for me to do now," Alma says.

Like the children, the adults move in and out of the rooms, though at a more sedate pace, as the moods take them. The bedroom is empty, except for the waterbed's frame. The bed itself has been emptied, and folded neatly into a case. At one point all the adults gather to sit on the floor of the bedroom, at others they gather round the table in the kitchen.

"Sure I'm going to miss Boston," Alma says. "I'm going to miss my friends and I'll miss the lights, because there's

31

not going to be any lights and stuff like that down there. There's gonna be nothing but crickets." Alma looks around. There is little else to pack, for Allied Van Lines will do the rest. The sense of dismantling her life suddenly hits her. "I am a little nervous 'cause I've been here like six years," Alma says slowly. "It's kind of like I hate leaving here. I've adjusted to here and I've got a lot of friends here and down there we're going to have to readjust to everything and find jobs and stuff. Tavis has got to readjust his way of living as well as Arthur and myself. But . . ." She hesitates, and then the quick burst of defiance. "All in all I'm glad 'cause then I'm closer to my mother and I can get to see my own family more."

Alma's family is very large. She is the fifth of ten children, and it is only after some thought she can give me their names in order, and even then she has to make a few corrections. Her family is divided between Memphis and Boston, except for one sister, Grace, who lives in Italy.

"Her husband's a soldier," Alma explains. "She doesn't like it much. She writes often to Mama who gives us all her news." She shakes her head in some disbelief. "I'd love to go to see her. Just get on a plane and I'll be there. How long does it take?"

"About eight hours."

"I've never ever flown in my life." She glances at Arthur as if he is to blame. "We drive everywhere, and I'm sick of that. I'd like to go see her for two weeks. Maybe longer. Maybe I'll stay there forever. What's Italy like?"

I start to give a quick picturesque and political sketch of Italy. Of Rome and Florence and the Via Veneto and bombs and assassinations and a sagging economy.

"I mean what's it like for black people?" Alma interrupts impatiently. "It's got to be better than here."

"Right on!" The chorus from around the kitchen table is exuberant. The beer is going down well; the half-gallons of whiskey and vodka and gin are nearly empty. These are the remnants of the party Alma threw the weekend before for all her Boston friends. Sixty turned up to drink to their health.

Alma, and this kaleidoscope of friends and relatives, of dark, gracious strangers to me, does not view the world in terms of cities and art, of history and cultures and political turmoil. The Vatican, the Forum, the great cathedrals of Italy, are swept aside as just so much artifice; camouflage that does not reveal the only reality of importance to her. Her perspective, like the path of a bullet, is narrow. She only views the world over the gunsights of her race. It is a collective, not a personal, vision. She is not Alma, but a people. Her experiences are their experiences. Her rejections, her failures, her success, her sadness, her happiness, even her thoughts are one and the same. This is not to deny her an individuality. She is certainly Alma: unique, pretty, capricious, acutely observant.

"I don't think Italy has racial problems. But that's because there isn't a big black population there."

"What does Grace think of Italy?"

"She thinks it's okay," Alma says. "Except she's homesick for the family. So when I wrote her I told her I'll be coming soon. We're going to tour around. We'll go to Germany and France and England and . . ." She ticks off the countries of Western Europe.

"It's gonna cost money," Bear says practically. Bear, like Doc, though they've lived in Boston longer, still speak with southern accents.

"You don't think I'm going to be a poor nigger all my life, do you?" Alma's glance changes to a glare. Then she tosses her head. "I'm going to be rich one day." She looks around at the apartment with a sense of achievement. "I ain't done too bad since coming here. I remember my first job up here. It wasn't much, but it was . . . like a million dollars to me because I'd never made more than a dollar and eighty-eight cents an hour for working down there."

Everyone laughs. They all understand what it's like working "down there."

"We've all done sharecroppin', haven't we Bear," Paul the Vietnam Veteran suddenly says. "Shit." He chuckles as if it were a joyous memory. "I'll tell you how sharecroppin' works if you ain't done it. We all have; we all grew up together. It's easy. This white man'll have some land and he'll say to me I can work his land. We'll split the profits, he'll say, down the middle. So you got no money for nothin'. You go to his store and borrow for the seed, and for the shirt for your kid and for a glass of milk, and some food. An' you work all year, knowin' you owin' say five hundred dollars. At the end, when you done all that work, and got in the crop, you still owe him five hundred dollars. My mama used to make me shirts out of sackcloth. She made two. One she give the man for some food, one I had. Next year you start again, and when you finish you still owin' five hundred dollars."

"Yeah," Bear says gently in understanding. "That's the way it is."

"But I'd still want to go back," Paul continues. "It's my home. I understand it better. In the South you know your boundaries. You can push someone only so far, and then you got to step back. In the North, I don't know the boundaries. I don't know the line between me and the white man. It keeps changin'."

There is a constant ebb and flow of children, in and out of the kitchen. Tavis leads them in their games. Arthur who had been listening from the other room, and who's finished his packing, has disappeared.

"He's gone to get his car license renewed. He forgot about it," Alma says. And then, "Why don't you?" Alma challenges Paul.

"I will . . . we all will one day."

Everyone except Alma nods.

The South haunts them all. It's not mythical to them. It

is real. They are exiles, no different from those who've left distant countries and different cultures. They've clung together; nostalgic and often homesick. And yet, I find it difficult to understand. All they've spoken of is oppression and exploitation and suffering. These are—judged against a universal morality whether defined in the Constitution of the United States of America or in the United Nations Charter of Human Rights, or the writings of Rousseau or Sartre—political crimes. And like political exiles, they dream of change, and of return.

"I don't know what it was like three years ago," Alma says. "It may have changed, but I don't think so. A little, but not that much. It's going to be harder for us to get back adjusted down South. Down there the whites still think they are superior to the blacks. And the blacks down there look up on the white people as being God or whatever. If I go for a job, and a white girl goes for a job, even though I was more qualified she would get the job."

"You've got to know The Man before you can get a job," Paul says. "White men. Knowin' black men don't get you nothin'."

"Should you be going at all then?" I ask.

"Why not?" Alma says, giving me that glance which makes me feel I've asked the wrong question. "Arthur wants to go home, and I'm his wife. We're going to give it a try. I'm going to go to school there. I want to go to a business college. There's where you make money. Business. I want to try and get into politics too. I want to try and educate more black people to really realize that we have come a long way but we still have a long way to go to be equal to the white man. I think in the South many of the blacks down there get mistreated and they just don't care. They just let it go on because most of them are afraid to speak up and say what they think. They're afraid of losing their jobs or whatever."

At this moment, I can believe Alma. She has the energy and the fire to make changes. She has touched another world, different from the one in which she grew up, and those grains of confidence, of some equality have changed her. She cannot return to that passivity, that acceptance of inequality which she has told me about. I consider the alternatives open to her in this new life in the South that she is preparing for. She can revert, but she can't. She can change all she touches in the same way that what has touched her has changed her. Or if this becomes impossible, she can break. Or retreat.

The packing has finished by two in the afternoon, and Alma keeps ringing Allied Van Lines. They are supposed to have come and packed the furniture and emptied the apartment, but the man on the other end cannot as yet give a definite time when the van will arrive. The driver has some other work. The day drifts by with talk among the adults while the children play inside and outside. Alma and Mona take off to buy a few buckets of Kentucky-fried chicken, while the others play music and talk.

Arthur returns with his new license. It had taken him longer than he'd calculated as he'd also had to settle a few bills. We sit out on the porch steps keeping an eye on all the children. The car looks clean, and he admits shyly that he also went and had it washed.

"I can do the run in twenty-four hours," Arthur says of the coming twelve-hundred-mile journey to Eufaula, Alabama. "I've done it. I just get in and drive. Nonstop. It ain't tough. That's when I'm travellin' alone. Today we're goin' to get to Washington, and stay with some friends for the night, and then start out again tomorrow."

Arthur, I discover, in spite of his shyness and reserve, the almost contemplative quiet surrounding him, is an impulsive man. When he feels like doing something he does it. His trips South aren't that frequent; nor are they planned. He just gets in his car and drives. Nor does he apparently inform his parents in advance.

"I'm sort of glad you know," he says. "I don't dread

the fact that we're moving, not at all. I'm not goin' to have any problems readjusting to the South. I prefer a much slower pace than the city life myself. There's nothin' much to do there. There's one disco, one movie house. The nearest good place to eat in is Doulton, and that's fifty miles away. But I like shootin'. I shot a deer once, just near my place. I skinned it myself. But I got to admit I wasn't happy growin' up there. Everythin's far away, and as a kid I couldn't get around much till I was old enough to get myself a car. But I'm pretty sure we'll adjust." He falls quiet, almost dreamlike in thought. "I want to go home," he says suddenly and firmly. "My family wants me back there to take over the land."

It's nearly four now, and the huge Allied Van Lines truck carefully negotiates the narrow street, and parks perfectly outside Arthur's apartment house. Only the driver gets out. In the passenger seat is a testy German Shepherd. It snarls when we approach. Arthur smiles in delight. On the cab window is the same decal sticker as on his car: "If you value your life as much as I value this truck, don't fuck with it."

The driver, a thin, wiry black man, is going to shift their furniture all by himself. He had spent hours looking for labor but no one wanted work. It appears a daunting job for one man; amost impossible. The stairs are narrow and there is such a lot to be moved. Bear and Paul and Heywood help the man. Alma watches with some anguish. It wasn't all real before; she was just playing at packing. Now the man has come, and has numbered the furniture and begun humping her possessions down those stairs. Arthur comforts her in a corner of the kitchen, and then starts packing his car with their clothes. By the time he finishes, there is just enough room for Alma and Tavis.

By nine o'clock that night the packing is almost done. The apartment is bare, the dust already accumulating in the corners, eddying across the floor. The lights are brighter, harsher; the only shadows, sharp and dark, are those of the people. There's nowhere to sit now, so we all stand around, awkward and quiet. It feels lonely because of the sadness. Alma weeps. Her brother and sister and friends comfort and hold her in turn, as if they want to remember the texture of her skin and her smell.

Arthur is calm, though also not far from the edge of tears. We have been talking about the journey softly, and of our proposed meeting in Atlanta. It's been a sporadic conversation; strained, yet for him, necessary. He needs to talk; to drain the nervousness. At one point, I ask idly whether life has been fair to him, a black man born in the South. I don't expect a reply for until now Arthur hasn't revealed the same streak of anger as Alma. He has only spoken with affection for his past.

"I think America owes the black people, you know," Arthur suddenly says. "Because they brought the black people here against their will and they forced their white tradition on us, so we had to live by what white people said. It's still pretty much the same today, you know, like the white man makes the rules, he makes the laws and all."

He stares at me a moment, calm, courteous, as if the passion had never been revealed, and then moves away to Alma's side. Tavis is clinging to Alma's legs, also crying, but from exhaustion. Arthur picks him up, comforts him. It's the signal to leave as he moves to the door with Alma by his side. We troop down behind.

The night is a glare of street lamps and shapeless shadows; the buildings are silhouetted against a hazy black sky. A few of the neighbors who are on the street come to say goodbye. It's only a formality: they don't stay long. Arthur carefully lays Tavis down in the back seat; his head pillowed by dresses and suits. There is a last round of tight embraces, kisses, a mingling of all their tears for the others too are crying openly now.

They get into the car. Alma cranes around waving,

staring hard to retain this memory, as Arthur pulls away. We see her hand only as the brake lights glow deep red in the night, and then swirl away to join the stream of traffic. We wait a few moments, quiet and drained, and then disperse slowly, one by one, no longer held together by Arthur and Alma.

CHAPTER 4

Behold the Beautiful Land

". . . which thy Lord thy God hath given thee. Behold the land, the rich and resourceful land, from which for a hundred years its best elements have been running away, its youth and hope, black and white, scurrying North because they are afraid of each other, and dare not face a future of equal, independent, upstanding human beings in a real and not a sham democracy," DuBois said in his October 1946 speech to the Southern Youth Legislature.

Atlanta isn't the South. It feels like a city, any city, anywhere. The highways in and around it are vast, hurried, and only the signposts to Chattanooga and Montgomery and Columbus, Ga., distinguish this part of America from any other.

It is a city with nearly sixty percent of its population black, and they are visible not only on the streets and in the banks and hotels and at the soda fountains but even in the seats of power. There is a black mayor and a black vice mayor. Half the city council is made up of black members, and a black man is head of the school board.

There is even a black sitting as head of the chamber of commerce.

And yet, all this is only an illusion of power, of political strength. Only three percent of Atlanta's economy is controlled by blacks. Real power has always been money, and this still remains in the hands of white people.

Yet, there is something familiar about Atlanta. Like Boston, it is a city of colleges. There are five in all, including Atlanta University and Morehouse College.

Morehouse has a beautiful campus. On a sunny, fall afternoon, with the leaves thick on the ground and the great square surrounded by solemn brick buildings, it is reminiscent of Harvard Yard. There are not as many students around, and the only sign of activity is a group of youths. Five are in uniform marching to the commands of three or four of their casually dressed elders. The five in uniform look like freshmen being initiated into a fraternity. They are all black; there isn't even the token sprinkling of whites here. It isn't reverse segregation, I'm told, but a social choice by white students. If there were a white male or female student who would they date, court, marry? They prefer to attend the white colleges where they will not be presented with such social problems.

There was a great struggle to establish schools, and later these colleges, and much of this early work was done by white liberals who established Quaker schools and missionary schools. Ironically, because of segregation in the South, black colleges and universities proliferated and today most of the black men and women who hold positions of leadership in America graduated from one of these Southern universities. In the North, because of the so-called desegregation, few blacks attended the great white universities.

The most famous graduate of Morehouse College was Martin Luther King, Jr. Doctor King was a native Atlantan. His presence is physically visible. Morehouse named its chapel after him, and Atlanta one of its highways.

"I think people will always have a memory of Martin Luther King," Alma says as we begin to work our way through Atlanta traffic. "He did so much to improve the black situation in Atlanta. They won't forget him where I come from either. He worked hard in Memphis to give blacks a better chance in their job situation."

"I think he died before he should have," Arthur says. "I wish he were still livin' today. I think if he hadn't been killed, the black nation itself would be advanced further than it is today."

"Can you remember where you were when you heard he'd been assassinated?"

"In school," they both reply. Neither can remember the details of the day that clearly.

We are traveling south on Route 85, an eight-lane sweep of concrete which imposes a harsh order on this beautiful land. I can see what DuBois meant, and can better understand Arthur Dean's love and yearning to return. Atlanta swiftly becomes a memory.

The day is warm. It is the kind of warmth, when the body is tired of cold and cruel winds, that one wishes to retreat to. It has only the slightest moist touch of heat; not enough to curse; just enough to open the shirt and throw the jacket on the back seat. The sky is clear, and the blue not so delicate as in the North. It is richer, deeper; a child's exuberant crayon could have shaded it. The light is clear with that different quality—sharper, somehow more alive—that one finds only in warm lands.

From Route 85 I catch glimpses of Georgia. The stands of timber, an almost blood-red earth, peanut fields stretching from the fence posts to the dip in the horizon, green fields dotted with cattle. From a sudden rise, the half circle of the horizon. The land rises and falls as if it's breathing. A hill of forest, a shallow valley of fields, the brilliance of water. Apart from the occasional house and cluster of buildings it is the superimposed discipline of the fields, the straightness of the divisions, that confirms the presence of man.

Eufaula is about one-hundred-eighty miles south of Atlanta, and just across the border, the Chattahoochee River, from Georgia. It is too long a drive without a break, and when we cut off on Route 27, down past Columbus, Georgia, we look for a restaurant. There are only those fast-food joints. They are garish; reds and blues and greens, revolving signs and hurrying neons, hamburgers and pizzas and fried chicken.

We choose the least unattractive. The lunch counters may be open, but the reception is cold and hostile. The plastic hospitality of "Good morning. How are you?," "Have a good day," and "Y'all come back you hear" isn't even whispered. The menus are dropped on the table, the eyes of this ancient waitress glitter behind her curving pink-rimmed glasses. She watches and waits.

Arthur and Alma sit straight, as if unaware of this visual dislike. Tavis, sitting and chuckling, evokes no response from the woman.

I am not at all easy. The transition had been too sudden, and I am unprepared. My first impulse, the only defenses I have, is to overreact. I want somehow to return this hostility, and yet, it hasn't been overt enough. There is nothing to grasp hold of; no word, no gesture, just this stillness. It's not only her. The woman at the cash register, the half a dozen other, white, diners. My second impulse is to stalk out. But my retreat is their victory.

I glance at Arthur and Alma, trying to gauge and imitate their reactions. Their faces are . . . blank. There is that skin and those eyes and mouth; chiseled, lifeless, as if the artist could only capture a likeness and wasn't skilled enough to capture their essences, their souls. They have, in their own way, retreated momentarily.

The waitress takes our orders, takes the menus, and turns away.

Arthur raises an eyebrow; Alma lowers her head and

glances first at me, then at the receding back of the waitress. Her face is so eloquent; some disdain, a touch of disgust, even some humor.

"She sure don't like us here," Arthur says softly. "That's what it's like here. Once you cross from the Northern section into the Southern section, there are certain things that the white people do, you know, just to irritate the black person. They just want to see how far they can push us, and stuff like that you know. Like for instance, when the cop stopped me this morning and we was in Virginia. There was myself and a guy from Maryland. He stopped us both at the same time. He talked to the guy from Maryland real slowly. 'Hey boy, are you drivin' like that in Maryland, how come you want to drive like that here?' And all that mash you know. And this black guy just said, he just said . . . 'Yessir.' You know he didn't say nothin'. Just 'yessir, yessir'." Arthur laughs again, mocking. "I think people who never leave and stay in the South, they . . . they . . . still think that when the white man says somethin' they are supposed to heed what he says. They is afraid of what he can do to them, you know." The waitress returns, silently places the food in front of us, and leaves. "I've never said 'yessir' to a cop ever," he continues proudly. "I've been stopped often, and they wait for you to say 'yessir.' I won't say it. I'll never say it to them. And you can feel they want to do somethin' to you. They want to break you."

"Yeah," Alma says as she looks around. The decor of the restaurant, which I now begin to notice, is quite unmemorable. Just behind us, through large windows, is a swimming pool. The water is pale emerald. "It's a whole different atmosphere when you come from North to South. I don't have to tell *you*. You realize you're in the South when people treat you snobbish."

Snobbish? Yes, it is an appropriate word. A cultivated,

but thoroughly false sense of superiority. I would have used a stronger word, but I am not Alma or Arthur. Although Alma did turn to me and use the conspiratorial "you," and we are the same color, I cannot duplicate their history or their emotions in this land. I am no stranger to racist slights, the mindless, stupid violence, a dart plucked suddenly from thin air, and hurled when least expected. There is no growing used to it; there are no defenses. We are similar in that respect.

I can get no closer than that for I recognize that the people in this room are ancient enemies. They have for centuries circled and probed and thrust; they know each other's strengths and weaknesses; they can recognize the signals of hostility and of the truce. They are practiced in the subterfuges of two weary fighters trapped since the beginning of their time in the same ring.

"Coming from North to South is . . . you feel like you have to get yourself readjusted to Southern ways," Alma continues, "instead of trying to keep your own pace to what you was doing in the North. I think in some ways it's hard for a Southern white to adjust to a Northern black. Because they say we speak out, we speak what we're thinking rather than keep our mouths shut like Southern blacks do. The whites expect us to just fall in place and do everything they tell us. I've discovered you can't just fall into place and do what every individual does. You have to do what you want to do in order to get somewhere in the world. You got to make up your mind and . . . like I come from a very poor family and know what it is to be really down at the bottom and I know the way that the whites used to treat me before I come to the North. So I don't want to fall in place no more. I'm going to do what Alma wants to do."

"Could it be dangerous?"

"Could be, but you have to take a chance."

We pay our bill, leave no tip, and go back out in the

warm day. Our mood has changed. It is quieter, reflective, even watchful. Ten minutes of silence, and then a diatribe.

"Black people," Alma continues in the car, "are simply afraid to move up in the South. For instance, my father was stopped about two years ago for speeding. They arrested him, and abused him and when he got to court he was afraid to say anything because he knew what they do to black people down there. So he stayed right in his place and said 'yessir.' He comes to Boston to be with me a while, and we was trying to get him on disability. My father's like my brothers. I said, 'Why didn't you speak up for yourself?' And he said, 'I'm afraid of white people, I'm afraid to say anythin'.'"

She sounds angry. Not so much at the whites, but more at her father. A bold daughter's respect for her parent must have been shaken by the confession.

"It hurt me when he said that," Alma says after a long pause. She is no different from any other child. Our first heroes are our parents, and what happened to her father must have diminished her respect for him. It must have been difficult for a rebellious black child to hold on to a respect for his or her parent over two centuries of slavery and one of social inequality.

"I'll never let Tavis be hurt like that," Alma adds.

Eufaula isn't far now. The highway has become a two-lane road; the land is closer, more immediate. The road is like a roller coaster—hill, valley, hill, valley. On either side, for miles, are dark, brooding trees. They are thickly foliaged, spreading, squat. From their branches and up along the trunk clings a feathery, eerie gray moss. It seems to be suffocating every tree with its gentle embrace. It makes the woods alongside look ghostly, even in the sunlight, and the deep shadows beyond, flecked with patches of sunlight, even more mysterious.

"Oak," Arthur Dean says laconically. "That stuff's always been on it."

Often the woodline breaks to reveal pastures with small herds of Brangus grazing, and once only, a cotton field.

"There you are," they both say triumphantly.

All I can see are rows of low bushes, speckled only here and there with white. I had expected more.

"It's been plucked," Alma says expertly. "Most will have been by now." She turns around, mocking. "You got to try it one day. It's easy. You just get your sack, and twist the bud off and put it in your sack. You go down one row and then back up the next and then down and up, and when you figure you have a hundred, you take it to The Man. He weighs it, empties it, gives you back your sack and you start off all over again." Her smile twists. "I sure ain't going to do that ever again."

"Is picking the same as chopping?"

"You don't know nothing," Alma says in disgust. "Chopping's different. You got this kind of hoe, and like you got to chop the ground between the bushes. Clearing the earth and dead leaves and stuff."

The traffic on the road is light. An occasional pickup passes by, now and then a truck. We pass small towns that appear to have been plucked from a Ray Stryker photograph. A gas station with a couple of old black men on the porch in rocking chairs watching the traffic go by; a store with a couple of old white men talking; a church, small, wood-framed with a cross stuck precisely on top of the roof. Every building is painted white, and there are never more than half a dozen structures before the fields and woods begin again. In each little township, the people appear to move, occasionally. From rocking chair to pump, from the store to across the street. A dog loafs along, tagged by children, white, while later we saw a group of black kids sitting in the shade. The two colors never appear in close proximity to each other.

But the land is always there behind them. Pretty fields, sloping woods, water sparkling through the trees. It's a rich land, in spite of the lack of rain. There has been a

47

drought for the last few months, but it is only infrequently that one notices this. Here and there the grass is worn like the bald spot on a man's head, and the breeze will suddenly catch a handful of dust and whip it up into a fine brown mist.

Soon Eufaula is only a bend in the road away.

CHAPTER 5

Comin' Home

The road widens suddenly past the curve, and slopes down. To the left is a fairly large lake, surrounded by a stand of trees. The water is still, a deep blue that is darkening with the sky. To the right are motels, a couple of bars and restaurants.

Arthur points to one bar as we pass.

"You don't go in there," he says. "It's white only. Last . . . last time I was here a couple of blacks went in and got beat up."

Once we pass his landmark, Eufaula becomes a beautiful little town. We drive slowly through broad, tree-lined avenues, and it is like taking a journey back into the Confederate past. Everything here looks as if a deliberate attempt has been made to still time and bottle it. Many of the homes are antebellum mansions. One, the Shorter Mansion, now a museum, is magnificent. It has high, white, free-standing Corinthian columns, and a porch that runs right around the building. There is a small curved balcony above the front room, and shuttered windows. The other houses are only fractionally less grand, each in its own way, whether antebellum or Victorian or gabled. They stand well back from the road and all seems well maintained. It appears, as we float past these ancient homes, to be a wealthy little community. They evoke a gracious, leisurely world of manners, strategems, flirtations, and of a false sense of honor and chivalry.

Eufaula—the name of an Indian clan—was founded in 1832, when the Cree Indian Nation ceded the land to the United States. The earliest white settlers, who came prior to 1832, were welcomed by the Eufaula clan, but as they began to set up trading posts and crude homes, the Cree Indian war broke out. The intermittent warfare between the Indians and the settlers lasted until 1837, when the power of the Cree Nation was finally broken and the tribes were shipped off to Oklahoma in the new Indian Territory.

Once the Indians were removed, the town began to boom. The economy was based on land, cotton and slaves. At one time there were nearly twenty thousand slaves working the plantations around Eufaula. The whites only numbered around seven thousand five hundred. During the cotton-rich years of the 1850s, planters shipped thousands of bales of cotton from the Eufaula wharfs downstream to Apalachicola. With the coming of the Civil War, Eufaula became a hotbed of seccession, and every family contributed to the Confederacy. Fortunately for the physical structure of the town, the war ended with the Union Cavalry just outside Eufaula.

The Reconstruction was a difficult era for the town because of its commitment to the Confederacy, but by the 1880s, it had managed to pick itself up again. The first cotton mill, Eufaula Cotton Mill, was established in 1888, and this became Eufaula's largest employer for decades. And until the first world war, very little change took place in Eufaula.

Since the '60s, however, Eufaula, in its own genteel way, began to boom. A dozen new industries moved in, and one company, American Builders, made Eufaula its corporate headquarters.

In Eufaula itself, there is little sign of these industries. The whole town could be a National Heritage. (Later I learn that there is a very active Eufaula Heritage Association which ensures that everyone keep these gracious houses in excellent order. And if I'd come in April, the past would have come to life. The white ladies and gentlemen dress up in their 18th- and 19th-century costumes, throw their homes open to the public, and hold balls and soirees. The black men dress up as coachmen, and the black women as mammies.)

Arthur's home is nine miles further south. We pass a monument of a Confederate soldier carved out of Italian marble standing on top of the thirty-five-foot granite column, and then an impressive, and monolithic Methodist church, one of twenty-eight Catholic and Protestant places of worship available for the town of twelve thousand people. Churches represent not so much the might of God, but the prosperity of their congregations, and this one looks as if it has a monopoly on the Eufaula rich.

The church stands at the crossroads of a commercial street. The stores look western: two-story, wood-framed, flat-fronted. White and black pedestrians stroll slowly along the sidewalks.

"Well, that's downtown Eufaula," Alma breaks the silence.

She sits with her arms folded, almost huddled.

"There's no comparison with Atlanta, is there?" Arthur asks. He feels more at ease. "Eufaula is the South. It has more of the image, hasn't it? Atlanta has a Northern image for me. Here, all you can think of and see is the South. All the surroundings is the resemblance of what the South was before. And what it should be like."

We dip past a railroad track, and enter a familiar era.

51

For the next four miles, we pass fast-food joints, banks, and used-car salesrooms. The familiar monotony is broken by a lake on either side of the highway. It is all part of the same one at the beginning of the town. Lake Eufaula covers forty-five thousand acres and has an eight-hundred-mile shoreline. It is known in Alabama as the Big Bass Capitol of the World. There is everything around here for the American outdoor sportsman. Apart from fishing, there is hunting—water fowl, duck, goose, quail, turkey, dove, deer.

"You can adventure here," Arthur says proudly as we swing off Highway 431, onto two-lane Route 131. It is now only four miles to the Stanford home. The Stanfords as freemen are as old as Eufaula; the two have grown (or stagnated) together for a whole century. "When we settle I'm goin' to do some shootin' again."

"You call that adventure?" Alma says. "Killing poor things."

"That's adventure," Arthur insists, and for a few minutes they bicker over the definition.

The road is lined on either side with stands of pine trees. Here and there it breaks off to reveal grazing lands, an occasional house set well back from the road and a few trailer homes much nearer. The road curves and dips gently, and at exactly the fourth mile, Arthur Dean slows and turns off onto a narrow dirt road to the left.

The lane runs straight for a couple of hundred yards, then as it passes a small, sagging house with a couple of mongrel dogs that give chase to the car, it swings right. At the bottom of a dip, we turn left into Arthur's home.

The house is away from the entrance, past the shade of two pecan trees. For about fifty yards, the land on the right, waist-high with grass and weeds, slopes down into a thick undergrowth of bushes and trees. To the left, dividing the Stanford property from their white neighbors is a sagging barbed-wire fence. A large yellow Barbour County school bus is parked just beyond the end of the weed patch; beyond that is a small wooden workshop, its timber brown and worn, and the windows nonexistent. Behind it is a dismantled pickup, with its engine on the ground. Further to the right, are several more dismantled cars, and a couple of swings. One is a tire hanging from a rope. Half a dozen chickens peck and scratch at the dusty earth and scatter at the approach of the car. Arthur Dean parks a few yards short of the house.

The house is made entirely of wood, and stands on brick pillars three feet off the ground. It is one-story, with a sloping shingled roof, about thirty feet wide and sixty feet deep. The stairs leading up the porch are planks; one is missing. The porch is cool and shady. There are a chair-swing to the right that could hold three adults, and two old and comfortable rocking chairs that face towards the road. On either side of the wire mesh door are windows. The curtains are drawn behind them. It is impossible to tell how old this house is. It could have been built a hundred years ago, and constantly repaired and nurtured. It feels as permanent as the land and the trees and as much a part of it. The wood is bare and weather-worn, and the whole house could do with some paint and a couple of nails here and there.

Arthur ("Bud") Stanford and Odie come out of the house and in turn embrace their son, their daughter-in-law and their grandson.

Bud Stanford is a tall, slim man in his early sixties. His skin is pale brown, suggesting only a suntan and this impression is heightened by the color of his eyes. They are a fine, pale gray; as delicate as a cloud on a fine evening. There is one other immediate quality in his eyes: steadiness. They never flick away, and are considerate and gentle. His voice is quiet and unhurried, with pauses, not of hesitation, but of thought. He wears a red peak cap almost continuously, and the hair below the edges is turning gray and the face has begun to seam. He has high cheekbones, and a strong mouth and jaw. Another permanent feature in his face is the cigar clamped in his mouth; chewed, but seldom lit. He has a firm, dry handshake, and his palm feels calloused. Bud is wearing a khaki shirt and trousers, and worn, brown work boots.

Odie doesn't look much younger than her husband. She's darker, more animated and emotional, and her love for Arthur is obvious. She has a round, strong face, and alert brown eyes, and her prettiness is still easily discernible. Odie is shorter than Bud, heavier and rounder. She looks like a woman who has worked hard and long, and has had little time for the luxury of daily pampering. Though she gives the impression of constant energy—she talks faster than Bud, she's full of gestures, her face is full of expression—you can feel the stillness under that surface. She is of the land, of the same solitude that surrounds her. She seems a comfortable, warm woman. A mother.

On the porch now are four young children. Three are pretty, cheeky-looking girls, who look so much alike that they must be sisters. They are: Patricia, Joanie May and Villain. The fourth is a teary boy of not more than four or five who weeps uncontrollably until he's picked up by Bud. The four are foster children who live with the Stanfords. Keith, the boy, is treated as if he were another son. Arthur's two sisters aren't at home. The elder one, Agnes, is married, and lives in Eufaula. The younger, Denise, is at college in Montgomery and returns home every weekend.

Odie has prepared a welcome-home dinner. The house is cool and dark. A hallway runs from the front door to the rear of the building, and on either side are rooms. Near the front door is a large frame with three photographs. In the center is Martin Luther King, Jr., and on either side, the Kennedy brothers. The bedrooms are on the left, and to the right is the living room. An upright piano stands against one wall, and a stereo set across the room from it. There are countless photographs: hanging

54

on the walls, on the coffee tables, on the piano. One is outstanding. It is of two elegant, handsome black men, sitting and looking straight into the camera. They are Arthur Dean's two grandfathers. The other photographs are of the more immediate family. Arthur and Alma, Agnes, Denise, Bud and Odie at their own wedding.

"Denise is the one that plays," Odie says proudly. "Sometimes, we all sing along when she's playin'." Odie's Alabaman accent is thicker than either Arthur's or even Bud's, and because she speaks quickly, I find it difficult to follow at first.

"We sing Gospel mostly," Alma says. She's been subdued for the last half hour. Arthur is very relaxed; Alma slightly edgy, an outsider. Her spirit, however, is still there. "Of course I sing. Before I left from the South I was the lead singer in my choir, and I was also the director. I'm thinking of going back to that here. Maybe."

"And I'll play the guitar," Arthur adds. "I got one, but I don't play that well as yet. I'm learnin'. Lot a good musicians have come from the South."

Arthur's, Alma's and Tavis's room during their temporary stay is at the back, behind the kitchen. It's a small room, crowded with a huge double bed and a dresser. Alma looks forlorn. Her world has shrunk from a two-bedroom apartment to this cubicle.

The kitchen is the heart of the house and the largest room. The dining table is groaning with the weight of the food. Ham, chickens, sweet potatoes, candied yams, two cakes, fresh bread, pies, spaghetti and meat balls, long greens, carrots, a bowl of salad and a pitcher of lemonade. There is enough to fill the stomachs of an army.

"My son is finally home," Odie says as she hands Arthur the first plate. For her, some silent prayer has been answered.

CHAPTER 6

Bud and Odie

The front porch doesn't run to the same width as the house. It falls a few feet short on either side and its roof, covered by aluminum sheets, slopes gently downwards. It takes three strides to cross from the front door to the five steps leading down to the dusty earth. The plank floor of the porch is uneven, with many gaps which, though not that wide, give one the opportunity to spy on the busy life of the chickens underneath.

To the right of the front door is a small hanging garden of potted plants. In contrast to the field beyond them, their leaves are green and fresh, instead of the baked brown of the grass. Beneath the plants are a kitchen table and an outdoor barbecue and an old television set and a rocking chair. Nearer to the door is another two-seater rocker. To the left of the door is a swing. It faces the plants and the field. It is not an elaborate swing. It is straight-backed, hung by slim chains to the beam overhead, and has enough space to sit two comfortably; a third would have to be a child. Beside it, and nearer the

56

door is a small rocker. A carton of empty 7-Up bottles stands on the edge of the porch. They've been there some time as if someone had placed them meaning to return them to the store, and completely forgot about them. They are now quite invisible to the inhabitants of the house, as is the old heater near the steps.

The porch is an ideal thoughtful person's study. Its clutter is natural; its simplicity harmonious with the surrounding landscape. The furniture on the porch is designed for long and dreamy hours of thought. The swing, generous in its space for one, requiring only an occasional push with a foot, can almost slow the heartbeat to its own creaking rhythm.

From the swing, the view, except for two man-made structures, is only of the rise and fall of the earth. The open field, through the leaves of the potted plants, begins a few yards from the edge of the porch. There is a barbed-wire fence dividing the Stanford land from that of their white neighbors. The farther side of the field dips into a thicket of trees, but just before that is a small house, almost an exact replica of the Stanford home, down to the weather-beaten planks and the tar paper roof. It looks unused; as if it will slowly settle into the earth and become a part of it, like a fallen log growing lichens and moss and grubs. About a hundred yards in front of that house is another. This one is on the edge of the dirt road leading to the Stanford home. Though made of the same materials and from a similar blueprint, it looks larger. There are a few mongrel dogs lazing around its yard, and though washing can be seen on the line stretching between two posts in the backyard, there is seldom sign of any activity. Now and then a dog will move from one patch of shade to another.

In between the neighbor's house, and the Stanford front gate is a low, long barn. It is across the dirt road, and houses one tractor and a plough. Beyond the barn, the open field rises to meet the sky. Once the field was planted with cotton, but now it only grows scrub grass. To the left of the front gate and right around to the rear of the swing, the view is more immediate. Near the gate is a large patch of tall grass, nearer is an old work shed under a pecan tree. On the other side of the tree, and nearer the house, are the children's swings.

I begin to understand why Arthur yearns to return to this place. The silence is composed of tiny, subtle sounds. It has to be listened to carefully for otherwise it sounds as simple and soothing as the sleep of a child. The darting sharp buzz of insects and bees, the leaves polishing each other, the quick crackle of a squirrel searching the earth for nuts, the breeze ruffling the grass, the flutter of a bird taking wing. Far, far above in the sky a hawk circles and circles and circles. Minutes and hours no longer become a valid measure; time has become a vast expanse of space.

Odie comes out of the house with Keith. He holds onto her with quiet intensity. He is no higher than Tavis, yet his troubled look gives him the appearance of carrying all the burdens of the world on his little shoulders. He anxiously watches as Odie walks to the rocking chair and seats herself; immediately he climbs onto her lap. Odie embraces him and turns to me.

"His mother's in Montgomery," Odie says. "She's tryin' to study there. He's been with us twice, and each time he gets used to us, she takes him away. I'm prayin' she's goin' to leave him with us now for a few years. I really love him." She looks at him lovingly and gently pats him on the head.

Tavis, chewing a piece of toast, comes out to consider his grandmother and Keith. Suddenly aware that she is about to talk, he sits on the top step of the porch and looks at her quietly.

She stares beyond the porch and slowly begins to intone the history of her family. They were from Alabama and she was raised not more than two hours away from where we are sitting. It becomes apparent that she is the historian of the Stanford family as well. Both families are deeply entrenched in and around Barbour County.

"My mother's name was Syllar Belle Morris, and she came from around here. Not far in fact, just over that rise," Odie begins. Keith has become restless and to quiet him she starts to comb his hair. Tavis, having finished his toast, wanders around the front yard. "My father was James Thomas Deeds. He was born and raised and he died workin' on the Deeds plantation, ol' T.T. Deeds' plantation, which isn't more than two hours from here. His mother's name was Teressa Deeds. I never knew her. On my mother's side, my grandmother was Arrie Lee Jones, and her husband was William Morris. I never knew either of my grandparents and nobody told me anythin' about them. My father, Thomas Deeds, died young, and my mother remarried. My mother's dead. She's been dead round eleven years. After I married, she became feeble and she and her husband, well, they moved in the house with us, and she lived here until she died. And her husband, he was sick at the same time. I was workin', we wasn't rich, we was poor people, and she lived here and I worked every day and come home and cooked and fed 'em. She was on one bed, and my stepfather on another, and my husband's mother she was also feeble, but she was up on her feet walkin' around, but we managed and we waited on them."

She is interrupted by Keith. He wants still more attention and starts to cry. Odie cradles him, feeds him a biscuit taken from her pocket, and he quiets. Beyond the pecan tree, we can see a young white man leaving the neighbor's, the Fairclough's house. He strolls over to the low barn, climbs into the tractor seat and starts it up. The burst of the engine grates against the silence.

"That Robin Earl," Odie says. "He didn't know how to read or write, till my Arthur (Bud) taught him how. The Fairdoughs used to be friendly to us one time. They'd say 'hello, how are you?' and once when Mrs. Fairclough got sick I took care of her. Then one day, we have a party line on our phone, and we hear her talkin' to some people, and she's callin' us dirty niggers." Odie falls silent, and shakes her head. "I don't understand. That hurt; but it was only after her husband died she did that." She shrugs it away, although the pain and the puzzlement still remain. "Oh well . . . I've been workin' all my life," Odie says. "I did a lot of field work, day work, and I did a lot of housework. I've been workin' since I was thirteen years old, doin' a lot of housework for different people till I was twenty-five. And then I worked in the fields at home, and that was extra from the work I was doin' at home to help support my mother and my three nephews. Their mother died and left them when they was quite small. I did most every kind of work in the field except plowin'. I never did plow a mule, but I did drive a tractor for a few hours, but I didn't do too much plowin' with it. And then I worked at Mann's bait shop makin' those aritificial baits you know, and once I worked at the dry cleaner, pressin' dry goods you know. I didn't do washin', just pressed them. I was then cookin' at school and keepin' foster children at the same time. And then I cooked at, it was known as, Riverdale Fish Camp, at the time I was cookin', but now it's gone. He's Mann's Steak House, I believe that's what it is."

Having finished combing Keith's hair, she lifts him off her lap to the floor. He looks as if he's about to cry but she hushes him, and calls to Tavis. Tavis ambles over, his knees dusty from playing in the yard. He obviously knows the routine for he comes and turns his back on her, so that she can plait his fine, short hair.

Her recital moves me. I am sadly reminded that the poor can never cease the struggle to survive. I have never believed there is much dignity in backbreaking labor. I have seen it degrade and destroy the poor in my country. It crushes all hopes and dreams and reduces men and women to mere draft animals.

I am surprised by the pride with which Odie has told

me her history. I had expected her to be bitter, enraged, to feel cheated by her life circumstance for she has little to finally show for all her labors. None of the things which the American Dream claims are the rewards for those who believe in the ethic of work. I recognize my own good fortune, and the extraordinary distance I have from these people and try harder to understand how those years of work have built the foundation that holds the family soul together.

Odie continues her story, her face expressive of satisfaction with her hard-earned accomplishments. "I was always able to get a job and work, and everywhere I worked I feel like the people had wanted me back again. I don't feel I was ever a bad worker for everywhere I worked, I have had compliments on my work. I did housework from the time my younger brother married and left me and my mother 'cause I helped support the family at the time. My mother didn't work away from home 'cause in those years the woman didn't work away from home too much. But I did housework to help support the family till I got married. I worked for four dollars and a half a week. I didn't look for a lot of money to spend, because I knew my mother couldn't support me and I had to help support the three children of my aunt. There have been some places I've worked in . . . well . . . they wanted the blacks to go round and come in, and they wanted you to eat at a different table. But at most places I worked I was treated as just one of the family, and when I was goin' home they would tell me I could take my food home, my dinner you know, with me and me and my mother could eat together, you see. But in the places where they asked you to go round the back and come in, I didn't work there long, 'cause I hadn't been used to goin' to the back. I had been workin' round white people all my life, and I'd go in the door they went in. I'd been treated like that all the while. They always treated me nice." She has pride in her face.

As she pauses she sees that I am troubled by the spare

litany of her life. I am curious why she has not wanted more, why she tells a story that seems devoid of dreams. She reveals little, except a calm acceptance that life wasn't supposed to have any further expectations. Dreams are white, and work is black and for Odie that's the way the world works. She has been well inculcated into that philosophy, even though a century has passed since her people had been freed. Instinctively, she answers the question I am unable to phrase.

"Well, the white man always had more," Odie says, "than the black 'cause it comes from slavery times. The black man had to labor for what he got while the white man inherits his from slavery times, you see. They had everything during slavery times, so the black man has come a long ways I think. They have inherited what they got since they was free, although some of the whites don't think they are free. They think we ought to be slaves, right on, but I don't think the black will be slaves no more. Well, they won't get the jobs they want, but they will get somethin' to do. They won't go back in the fields and kitchens, like they once have. There has been a time when I thought things was goin' to get much better, but, you know, since there's been so much of changes in the White House, I don't know anymore. It's a little bit better than it has been, much better than it was when I was a child."

"What do you feel about the whites in Eufaula?" I ask, for Eufaula reflects little of the hardship, even less this gigantic struggle to keep alive. It's a different world, another nation. Those exquisite buildings only remain as a constant longing for what the white nation believes to be a glorious past. A past that needs to be merely imitated, not to be learned from.

"Eufaula is a kind of a prejudiced town," Odie says, pushing her spectacles up the bridge of her nose. "It wants to keep the best jobs for the whites, and the blacks takes the lesser jobs, the least-paying jobs anyway and the dirty ones. When it comes round to hiring to do the inside work in businesses, they mostly hire the white. The black takes the outside job. It's better than it was four or five years ago, because they do have to hire a few blacks, and these businesses can't run without them. It's not supposed to be a segregated town. The United States says that, but Eufaula is a segregated town. It exists. If a black girl or a black woman goes to be a secretary, they never hire one to be a secretary. They hire a white. They hire the black to do the cleaning, in my opinion, doing somethin' like that. But the secretary work and book-keepin' and all that, the black may be more capable of doin' it, but they hire the whites, and don't hire the blacks."

Every Saturday, Odie goes into Eufaula to do her shopping, and to meet friends. She enjoys spending the day in town.

"I don't feel black when I'm in Eufaula," Odie says, shaking her head. She has finished Tavis's hair and he climbs down the steps to the yard. Keith returns to her lap. "I feel like I'm just a human bein'. There is black and there is white, and I feel the black race is just as important as the white race. I don't feel I should be treated different because I'm black. There is some in Eufaula that thinks well of me and my family, and there is some that don't think anythin' at all about us. We are just blacks and they couldn't care less about us."

The silence settles. What was curiosity at the beginning of our meeting has turned, for me, into one of respect and affection. I like Odie's dignity and strength and intel-ligence. She has manged to live through a minefield of emotions without losing her perspective on life. Our silence is comfortable for me.

Keith tentatively leaves Odie to try to play with Tavis. Tavis is riding his tricycle and promptly runs into Keith who retreats in tears. Arthur comes out onto the porch, with a mug of coffee. He still appears tired after the long drive from Boston. He sits on the steps, watching Tavis riding his tricycle up and down a small slope under the branches of one of the pecan trees.

"I was in the hope that Arthur Dean would come back," Odie says as if her son isn't within hearing. She always calls him "Arthur Dean." She makes the name sound elevated, even though it is also to distinguish him from her husband, Arthur. "I hated so bad to see Arthur Dean leave. I wanted him to come back home. But at that time he wanted to go, you see. He was quite young, just turnin' eighteen, and he thought maybe if he went away he could get a better job because he was always real tiny and small. He thought it was goin' to be kind of hard for him to get a job here, and he said he wanted to finish his education. He wanted to work and go to school at night. Well, there was no school down here where he could go to at night, and work in the day so he went to Massachusetts. But he didn't go to school when he got there. Then after a few years he got married. I was prayin' for Arthur Dean to come back home because I wanted him close by. I don't know, seemed like I always had a . . . little different feelin' towards him about bein' away. I wanted him to be near home. The other children say I think more of him than I do of the rest of the children, but I love all of them 'cause they're all mine. But he looked, like, tinier than they was." Odie pauses and glances down at him with deep affection. Afthur stares out into the distance. "His health was good, but he was so little, and I just thought it might be better if he was to be close around. So after he say he was comin' home, I was glad to hear him say that. I hope he'll stay. I feel like he'll get a good job, and I feel like they can live well here. They may not make much money here as they was in Massachusetts, but at this time things are a little bit higher up there, because the cost of livin' is so much higher. They can live down here about as well 'cause the cost of livin's not quite as high. He can grow everythin' himself. He can grow his meat, his beef, he can grow his own bread, and he won't have to buy so much, if he manage it right."

I glance at Arthur. He appears not to be listening to his mother. He's obviously accustomed to being discussed this frankly. Tavis tires of his tricycle and comes to Arthur. After a moment, they stand up, and hand in hand stroll slowly up to the front gate. Arthur has a definite proprietary air. He's the prodigal, and that gives him a feeling of confidence and power. They pause often on the stroll while Arthur points things out to Tavis—a bird, the squirrels, a butterfly. Sometimes, Arthur himself has to stop—to examine a break in the barbed wire; or to pick up a pecan nut, open it, and hand its flesh to Tavis. They appear to be busy in each other's company.

"Arthur Dean's never been a rough, wild child," Odie says, watching her son and grandson exploring the grounds. "He was easy to handle because when you spoke to him, if he didn't like it, you didn't know it. Or if he liked it, you didn't know it. He's a little more solemn-minded now than he was, but he wasn't wild. I think since Arthur Dean's been to Massachusetts, that he feels that's enough for him to see. I think it's a good thing that he came home, after all his daddy's gettin' to be a little aged, and I'm also gettin' to be aged. It needs somebody to look after the livestock and other stuff we have here. Arthur Dean can do a lot of good here. He can see about that, he can get a job of work, and he can live at home."

She dreams the dream of all parents: the child is of age to become the protector, the father of his own parents. Like Odie before, becoming the mother to her mother and stepfather. It happens in most closely knit families; the past and the future are not a chasm apart, only a fractional break in the rhythm of time. Arthur, I realize, is held here by love: love for this land, for these people. He came because of them, and, if he can, he will remain because of them. It is also his sense of duty, his sense of responsibility; and these are difficult burdens to dislodge.

His parents in turn have conspired. They've promised him this land, the house, anything. The need, with the tiring of the body, becomes urgent.

But Arthur isn't alone, and Alma isn't Arthur. She is of a different age, and she nurses a different hunger. I doubt whether she can make this house her home. Not that room in the back, not without all her own possessions.

"I think Arthur Dean did well comin' back," Odie says. "He was born and raised here and he knows the people, and the people thought well of him, white and black. He never had no problem with the white and he didn't have no problem with the black. A lot of his white friends still ask about him now. I was afraid he might never return. I'd seen so many stay away, and I didn't want him to do that. I also thought he might get up there and get with a group of wild youngsters his age and get off and start drinkin' and smokin' and on dope, and he would just stay away. But I had taught Arthur Dean pretty good. I had told him to go to church and make the best of life, and above all I told him don't get onto drugs. Thank the Lord he hasn't got on it so far, I'm glad of that I think Arthur Dean will stay to his trainin' pretty good."

That part of her is instilled in Arthur. He never drinks or smokes cigarettes or touches drugs. I'm sure he doesn't go to church as much as she would like him to.

Arthur returns with the mail, and hands it to his mother. He turns to me. "You want to see the hogs?"

The hogs are in a long pen at the bottom of the slope to the left of the house. We stroll past the swings and the disemboweled pickup. He and his father intend to start work on it soon. The engine belongs to one of the other cars, and Arthur briefly sketches some of the technical difficulties involved in converting the engine to fit the pickup.

"It's easy," he finally says. "That's how I made my first car."

I know nothing about cars and I accept his judgment.

There is a barbed-wire fence, and we wriggle through. Tavis has little trouble. The ground drops steeply, and we can hear the piglets squealing. There are ten sows and four pigs, and a couple of piglets. In their nervous panic they remind me of Keith.

"Know anything about them?"

Arthur smiles: "Not a thing." He pauses, and smiles again. "I'll learn."

CHAPTER 7

Bud

Bud Stanford wakes daily before dawn. Oddie rises with him, makes him breakfast, and by six, accompanied by the three foster girls, he goes to work. He drives the Barbour County school bus to collect the children for the Baker Hill school. The route he takes twice daily zigzags over nearly half the county. Through highways, down dusty red dirt tracks, past fields of peanuts, cotton and soya, by thick woods and small farms. He stops at neat white ranch houses, trailer homes, and wooden shacks. Most of the black children he picks up live in a wilderness of fields and undergrowth, most of their homes unpainted wood shacks with tarpaper roofs. Their smaller brothers and sisters play outside. They are barefoot and dusty and shyly beautiful.

To my surprise not all the white kids live in those neat ranch houses set beyond the trimmed lawns. A few in the bus live in homes no better than the black kids.

"Oh yeah," Bud says as he drives around picking up the children, "when I went to school I had to walk, 'cause there were buses, but no black rode the bus at the time. We had to walk, rain or shine, cold or hot." He talks softly, with pauses, thoughtful. "We had to walk and if it was rainin' the bus would pass us sometimes and throw mud all over us. I never thought the time would come when I would be drivin' one. So now I'm drivin' the school bus. Of course, in them days, the whites went to one school and the blacks went to the other, and the white rode the bus and the black walked. But now they all go to school together, and I'm drivin' this bus." Bud, I suddenly realize, is very proud of this job. It has given him a sense of achievement. In a world in which he once expected no progress, it has suddenly catapulted him to a position of importance. "A lot of difference, a lot of difference. Quite a bit. And when I first went to school, we didn't even have a school building, we went to school in the church. That's where I spent my school days: in the church. And later they built a school. But now we've got the best school. There's a lot of difference, a lot of difference."

The Baker Hill school isn't more than a couple of miles from Bud Stanford's home, although by now he has driven thirty or forty miles. The school is well spread out with the classrooms grouped together on one side of a large traffic circle. Opposite, taking up nearly half a block, is a gym. Beyond are hills and fields. Arthur and Denise attended this school. The older children, Heywood and Agnes went to the T. V. McGhoo school in Eufaula. T. V. McGhoo was the only black doctor in the town. And since his death, there's been no other.

"There's a lot of difference," Bud says on our way home. "The superintendent now calls me 'mister.' It wasn't done before. The kids, black and white, are friendly towards each other. We've never had no trouble in Baker Hill school. They're all friendly. I grew up with a number of white people though I never went to school with them. Most . . . most of them was friendly, though some wasn't too friendly."

He stops the bus at a crossroad and carefully turns on the highway. After a moment's silence he adds, "But there was also a lot of coloreds, a lot of blacks, wasn't too friendly you know. It's still a long ways to go with the whites, but it's a lot different now. We don't visit too much still. I mean you can go in the house but not sit down in the livin' room and havin' a conversation. One or two places you can, but most of them you can't. You go on business or somethin', you tend to your business and then you leave. They won't ask you to come in, have a seat, drink some coffee. Nothin' like that. Well, may be now and then you'll find one that will, but mighty few. It's a long ways to go yet."

Bud parks the bus next to the patch of weeds in his grounds, and we walk slowly over to his porch and take the rockers. He sticks a cigar in his mouth, stares out at the trees, as if trying to remember what they look like. In the silence, I can hear the distant hum of a tractor working a field, the sudden surge of noise and then the murmur.

"You ever sat down at a white man's table?" Bud finally asks me.

"Yes."

"I never been invited to eat with a white man," he says with sadness.

Keith, having heard Bud's voice, peeps through the screen door first, and then comes out to cling to Bud's legs. Bud pulls him up on his lap.

I glance at Bud. There is no resentment in his face, nor was there in his voice. This simple act of breaking bread with another human, which I have taken for granted all my life, has been denied him. "Have any of your friends sat down at a table with a white man?"

Bud sucks on his cigar a moment. It is an extension of the expression on his face. "Not that I can think of.

"Well, I've never sat down at a table with a white man in the South.

"Some day black and white might live together and be neighbors," Bud says. "It'll probably be a long time. It might happen, but it will be a long time. Especially not as long as I live. It might happen before the end of my time, but I'd say it's goin' to be a pretty good while yet."

Bud Stanford's family originally came from a small community, Sandville, which is four miles from his home. The land which he owns today, one hundred and six acres, was bought by his grandfather, Robert Fantory, over a hundred years ago. His grandfather walked the eighty miles to Montgomery to register the purchase in the Alabama county records. On his father's side his grandfather was Joe Stanford, who owned no property. Fantory's daughter Emma inherited the property. Bud makes no mention of his father. His father left the family when Bud was two years old, and he never saw him since. Bud was brought up by his grandmother and his mother, who died three years ago.

"My grandmother used to talk about how she was brought up, slavery times," Bud says quietly, turning to me. "They couldn't go to church and no other places they wanted to, they couldn't go unless they—the boss—would let them go, you know. My grandmother told me when they were comin' up, if their boss saw another person they wanted, they would just buy like cattle, hogs, cows. And they would bet on them, put them on the block and bet on them, and they'd be sold away from the parents. Of course, she was never sold, she remained with her parents until after slavery, after freedom. Then she married off. No, she didn't tell me about her mother or father, except for the slavery times. And those were hard times."

We sit and rock awhile. I press gently for more details of his grandmother, but there is little more he can recall. She died when he was still a child. I'm not sure what I expect. It certainly isn't this abrupt termination of the past; it's as if nothing existed beyond his grandmother. I had expected a discernible connection to great-great-grandfathers, and great-great-grandmothers. It would be nearly impossible for the Stanfords themselves to reach back to their distant ancestor. The families were broken up too often. There was no communication between the sold slaves, no reading, no writing, no records. And somewhere in Bud Stanford's past there is a white ancestor, with those same pale gray eyes, who did not acknowledge or record the existence of his issue.

In the old history books on the South, the black man is invisible. He is there in the county records I study in Montgomery, and yet as a person, a human, he isn't. There is no mention of the births and marriages and deaths of slaves. In *The History of Alabama* (1862) by Albert James Pickett, the Negro is mentioned only as a statistic: in 1790, the "Children of the Sun" were first brought to the state; by 1820 there were 42,450 slaves; and by 1830, 117,549 slaves and 2,690 free black men. This book, like every other of that period, is only the history of the white man. It records his struggle, his prosperity, his battles, his hopes. Ironically, both white and black began on an equal footing at the very beginning. The whites were brought across from Europe as indentured servants by the companies which owned the plantations. However, they could work off their servitude over a period of years, and win their freedom.

"Well, I think the Stanford plantation was on the other side of Montgomery," Bud says quietly, ruffling Keith's hair. "I tried to check it out once, but didn't have no luck. And then I read somewhere that this university in California called Stanford were tryin' to trace all the Stanfords in the country. I wrote off and got me a form from them, but I never sent it back."

In between his two bus trips Bud works on the chores. He has to feed the hogs and tend the cows. He has a trailer park on the edge of his land by Highway 131, from which he receives some rent. The remainder of his income comes from his livestock. Every Friday, he drives over to Clayton to attend the market, and either buy or sell his livestock. The cows graze on the vacant land behind the house.

"I've got about forty to forty-two head of cows and calves together," Bud says as he walks down the steps to his hogpen. "I've only got fourteen swine. Sometimes, I have thought of earnin' more land and hogs and cows, but it takes a big effort to earn more. When the price is good, you can do all right with a big bunch of hogs, but when prices go down it takes all you can make to feed them. Feed is expensive. A cow mostly eats grass and they're not expensive, except in wintertime. But a hog eats high-priced food which costs about thirty dollars a hundred, and it takes a lot for a hog so if the price ain't right, you come out in a hole. But cows you can keep about eight to ten months and just let them eat grass and sell them off in the fall for about two hundred dollars a head."

His annual income, depending so much on the price of hogs and cows, is only marginal. Most of the land we walk over, with Keith in tow, is vacant. The soil looks rich enough to farm.

"Only a few white farmers grow crop," Bud says, stopping to pick at the earth. "But they're big farmers, they're rich folk, you know. They've got eight or ten tractors and three, four hundred acres of land, and they rent another three, four hundred acres probably. But they do good when they make a good crop, but when they make a bad crop it just bad. Black or white, it don't care what color if you make a bad crop. But I was always a little farmer. I never did plant over, say, one hundred acres, one hundred twenty-five. Maybe fifty acres in peanuts, and eight to ten acres in cotton and then the rest in corn. I made pretty good some years, some years I didn't do well. Of course that's what it's like farmin' a lot of the time. You don't make expenses."

My discovery of the nature of the South is gradual, often too gradual. I had been puzzled why Bud Stanford had completely stopped farming, even being a "little farmer." Farming to me, given all the hazards of nature, has been the act of plowing, sowing, reaping, and finally selling. The black farmers I speak to later are quick to explain the exact minefields they have to negotiate. It begins with the price of the seed and the fertilizer. Black farmers have to pay an inflated price for both, and if they turn out to be successful, they discover that the next year, the white storekeepers will sell them neither. "It'll be out of stock," one of the farmers tells me. And once they've harvested the crop, they have to sell to a white man who deliberately will downgrade the quality of their cotton or their peanuts or their soya beans or their tobacco and buy it at the lowest possible price. Later, he sells it at its original high grade.

I mentioned this to Bud later. He studied me for a long moment, and finally nodded: "That happens," he says quietly. "We try and fight that. When my children was little and there were civil rights marches in Eufaula and Clayton and Montgomery, I marched in them. I didn't go so far as Montgomery, but I did go to Eufaula and Clayton. I'd get into the march and march, and we boycotted Eufaula. They were surprised, but I think it done a lot of good. Things got a bit better after that. A lot of us went to jail. I didn't." He stops a moment, and then a bitter note creeps into his voice. "You know, all of us blacks were supposed to boycott the town, but then later I find out some of the blacks, you know, don't. They sneak into Eufaula and buy their stuff, and come and sell it to us. We had to buy 'cause we had nowhere else to go." It's now nineteen years later and the memory still hurts him. He can understand the enemy without, not the one within. "Oh I'm still involved with politics here. I work for the NAACP."

But today, we talk of other things. The day is hot, and we're sitting out at the back, his herds of cows behind us, the quiet, peaceful house in front, silhouetted against the blue sky. We put our feet up on the rusted plow, and Keith wanders, always within reaching distance of Bud.

"I wouldn't advise Arthur Dean to grow crops," Bud continues. "Cows and hogs is all right. He can make somethin' from that. But just croppin', unless he was a big farmer with a lot of money and was able to buy about eight or ten tractors and rent three or four hundred acres of land . . . well, I wouldn't advise it. It wouldn't be worth it."

There isn't an exact similarity between Arthur and his father. Physically, Arthur is smaller, frailer and his face doesn't quite match his father's. Arthur's face is more delicate in its outlines than his father's. But they are quite similar in character, and I can see where Arthur has inherited the same gentle voice, the courtesy, and the long calm quiets in any relationship. They also walk the same: a kind of rolling stroll, unhurried, as if all things will wait for their final arrival.

"Well, it was sad when Arthur Dean left but he was grown and I couldn't tell him what to do," Bud says. He lit his cigar, puffed on it a couple of times, and let it die. The thin, blue smoke hangs a moment, then slowly drifts away as if in search of better companionship. "I tried to advise him to stay down here but he wanted to go. He had a brother up there and he felt like he could make it and so I let him go. I felt he would have been happy here at home. I've been here all my days and I've been happy. Yeah . . . content." He smiles gently and stops a while to savor this feeling. "I did go up to Boston to visit. I just said 'it wasn't no place for me.' I think they was enjoyin' it, but I saw it wouldn't do for me to live there. I didn't like it, not to live. It was all right to visit, but I didn't like it to live. Arthur Dean's a lot like me. He likes this life."

And yet Arthur Dean, like millions of other black men who were born and raised in this beautiful land, needed to escape. First from slavery, and now from economic exploitation. It is always difficult to pinpoint the exact moment of an escape. There is no second or hour or day when a man in retrospect can say he needed to leave. Nor a particular thought or whisper or idea which is enough to set the mind, if not the legs, of a man running. He grows restless, uneasy in his mold, distrustful with his daily life. And once that happens, an innocence is irrevocably lost. He cannot return to those days, he cannot become what he'd once been because of the subtle shift in his thoughts and needs.

"Hayward has changed," Bud says with regret. "I don't know whether I can explain it or not, but he's just . . . he's a different boy. I can't hardly explain it, but he's a lot different than when he growed up here." He shakes his head slowly, considering the cigar in his hand. "I don't see much change in Arthur Dean now although most of them, their attitude changes when they go North and come back. I haven't seen too much change in Arthur Dean."

I do not know what Arthur was like before he left home. As he has such a close moral resemblance to his father, I presume that, if he'd not left, he would be another Bud. If I can see the similarities, I can also see the differences which Bud, because of love, his need for his son, doesn't. Arthur Dean has certainly been infected by his long stay in the North. Like any son wanting to please and love his father, Arthur Dean shields him from some of them. The simplest change is the obvious: in the North Arthur won more material success than his parents have had in their life. On another level there is his pronouncement, "America owes the black man . . ." He can no longer accept the same injustices as those perpetrated on his parents.

"Well, I don't think he made the right decision when he went North, but he thought he did," Bud says. "He said he was going to finish school up there, but he just went to work. Sure he done well, but later, when he decided to come back, I was glad. I think he made the right decision when he came home. I don't think it'll be no problem for Arthur Dean to find a job. He may not find just exactly what he wants to start with, but he'll find what he wants eventually. He was makin' out pretty good up there, and he may not make exactly what he was makin' there. But he'll make enough to live and be happy."

The light has begun to fade. Our shadows have become less defined, stretching, trying to float away to those pockets of darkness that have begun to form near the woods to our left. The air has also chilled. It won't become uncomfortably cold for another month, till December, but the change from day to evening is enough for me to slip on a coat.

"It snows sometimes down here," Bud says as we walk towards the house. "But most of all, we need rain. We keep prayin' for it, but so far it ain't come. It's the longest time we've been without rain for some years. Well, there's not much grass for the cows, and if I have to buy them feed, that's goin' to cost me a lot. I may have to sell them soon."

In the front of the house, Tavis and the three sisters are playing on the swings. Alma is pushing Tavis gently, almost lethargically. Villain, the youngest and cheekiest, brings over a collection of pecan nuts, and runs back to join her sisters on the other swing. Pecan nuts resemble walnuts but I discover that the meat is fatally delicious; especially when it's made into a pie.

"I don't think Alma'll have much trouble settlin' down here," Bud says, pulling himself up to sit on the edge of the porch. His legs swing, nearly dislodging a chicken. It clucks to safety deeper under the house. "I believe she'll find a job quicker than Arthur Dean will. I don't know, but I don't think she's been livin' in town all her days. She has lived in the country, and shouldn't find this a problem. I think one of the reasons most of our people, especially the black, go North is that they don't ever get the kind of job they want down here. They figure they can find a better job up North and a lot of them go by what they hear when other people come back and tell them what they've done. I don't know whether they are any happier or not. I doubt it." He says this almost wistfully, and I'm sure it's a wishful thought directed at Arthur and his brother Hayward.

"Arthur Dean will find the right job," Bud continues, with a surge of confidence. "It's better here now for the black man than it was when Arthur Dean left. Things have improved a whole lot. The black here can do most anythin' the white does."

The lights come on in the house. Pale square patches fall on the porch floor, touch our backs. The sky and the rise of land ahead, beyond the dirt road, have begun to merge. The trees nearby have begun to become indistinct and they are topped by the first faint specks of stars.

"There'll always be a problem between black and white," Bud reluctantly admits. "It might change some-day but not in my lifetime. Arthur Dean may live to see some of it. It was a big change from what it was when Arthur Dean was growin' up, it's a bigger change than what it was when I growed up. I don't know whether it'll ever be perfect. The black and white . . . there'll always be a little somethin' between them. That's just a fact of life. It don't bother me, but I guess I'm used to it. Of course, I'll do most anythin' I want to do, the color of my skin don't make much difference to me." He laughs, stands up and goes in for dinner.

Alma climbs the porch to take one of the rockers. I take

the other. Bud, I feel, is at peace. He has accepted a sense of the order of things, his place in life. He has fought his wars the best he can and shown great dignity. His needs, his ambitions, his wants, those insatiable furies that drive most of us, have been stilled. With age has come an understanding. Bud, like Odie, is aware of the huge imperfections in his life, and has learned to live within these limitations. And now the final gap in his heart has been filled. His son has returned.

"What do you think you'll be doing in a month's time?" I ask Alma.

She glances, looks away, looks back.

"What are you doing?"

"Sitting. Rocking."

"That's what I'll be doing."

CHAPTER 8

Settlin' In

Arthur's first act a couple of days after his arrival and once he's recovered from the long drive, the welcome of his father and mother, and the perceptible wriggle of settling himself back into the rhythm of their home, is to take his car into Eufaula for a wash and shine. My only surprise at this is that he didn't drive through a car wash when he first arrived in Eufaula.

It's past ten in the morning when he starts off. Bud has returned with the school bus and gone into town on "chores." Odie and Keith have gone "visitin'." The house looks untenanted from a distance. The children are in school, and only one or two chickens roam the front yard.

The quiet is pervasive. To listen to this continual silence, if you are a city person, is difficult. Nothing appears able to penetrate. A car horn is a forlorn sound; it is absorbed so quickly there isn't even time for an echo. We become accustomed to constant noise and crowds, and build up the barriers to preserve our personal space. And yearn for the solitude of a country retreat.

The distinction between solitude and loneliness is thin. It depends on the mind that views them; depends on the understanding of itself and on the nature of silence. This silence can heal, soothe thought, still the chaos of the outside world. It imposes and demands obedience. But here you are vulnerable and open to the universal infection of loneliness. The silence can search, pry and break open a man; force him to run for the comfort of companions, lights, noise.

Alma, dressed in jeans and a shirt, with Tavis trailing behind her, strolls around the yard. It is an aimless exercise, as if she decided to go for an exploration, and then suddenly discovered there was nothing much to explore. It must all be familiar to her own life in Tennessee. The dust, the heat, the silence. Tavis, however, seems to enjoy himself. He can run without coming up against a speeding car or a concrete wall. At first, I thought Alma had more control over Tavis. He seems to obey her, but when he decides he has no intention of listening to her, Alma has to call in Arthur. Tavis obeys his father a lot quicker than his mother.

"Yeah, I miss Boston, all the bright lights and stuff," Alma says. "But being back here is exactly what I'd expected. The only problem of living in the country, a place like this, is I can't go anywhere. I can't go shopping or take a walk in the town. You need a car, and we've only got one. And once Arthur gets a job, he's going to need it. Maybe we'll buy a second car . . . but that depends on how we do, don't it? I got to get myself a job as well. I hope that happens real soon. I like working."

For Alma, the return to the South has been a greater act of courage than for Arthur. She will have to make the greater effort to adjust, and to find friends.

"I don't know whether I can find any friends here. Most of the people around here are farming people. They work on the land. Yeah, cotton picking, peanut picking . . ." She trails off. These are the same people she fled years ago. "In the evenings here, like I plan a whole bunch of stuff for me and Tavis to do, to occupy our time so we don't get bored. First of all I'm going to take up music, and teach Tavis something too. Then I'm going to get active in the church again. I want to be like the assistant director in the choir, and I want to be secretary or something in the church. Most of all, I want to get really into community affairs. I didn't do much of all this in Boston 'cause I didn't have enough time to do it. Most of my jobs there were night jobs and when you're singing in the choir most of the rehearsals take place at night. So I never did it, but here I'll have the time. Lots of it," she adds, not sounding too pleased with the prospect.

A bright red car, with a white top and a deep booming exhaust, trails a cloud of dust down the road towards the Stanford home. It passes the gate, and then seconds later, backs up and turns in. A black man accompanied by a very prettily dressed little girl climbs out. He's an old school friend of Arthur's and he's heard that Arthur has returned. Arthur admires his friend's car and for half an hour they talk cars, prices, speeds, fuel consumption. Tavis and the little girl shyly make friends, and by the end of the visit they're playing on the swings. Shortly after they leave Arthur decides to go into town on a few chores. I ride with him.

"He's a soldier in Montgomery," Arthur says as we drive into Eufaula leaving Alma sitting in the rocker, watching Tavis playing. "He was just visitin' home. The only white friends I have here . . . are the ones I went to school with. And them I haven't seen in seven years. I think they'd be . . . friendly. There's one girl who works in the real estate office here in Eufaula, and before I decided to build my own house I thought of buyin' somethin' from her company. She was quite friendly when I went into the office. She recognized me right off, you know. So I think the other ones would be quite friendly too. But I don't know of any families here in Eufaula where black and white has sat down to have a meal together in their own homes. I don't know any." We turn off Highway 131 onto 431. The lake on either side is absolutely flat and calm. Around its shoreline, spaced well apart, I can see the still figures of fishermen. It's a perfect, lazy looking day for the sport.

"Well, the black people here in Eufaula still think the white man's superior, you know," Arthur continues. "And the white man here, he don't like . . . he don't mind bein' friendly with the black man in the street, but to invite him in his home I think is out of the question. They wouldn't like that at all. That would be just a little bit too friendly. Yeah . . . there's still two classes here. Black and white. As long as we stay in our section, and they stay in their section, things will keep workin'. But when you mix em' together . . . I don't think it'll work. They don't want that to happen. They probably would be afraid that may be their white children would become too friendly with the black people, and they would have intermarriage. Those white mansions you seen are important to them."

At the moment, those white mansions are a few miles away. On either side of us is the familiar evidence of fast-food America: pizza huts; hamburger stands and pancake houses. Arthur's first chore after washing his car is to visit the bank to discuss the loan he needs to build the house on his family property.

The United Federal Savings and Loan Association is a neat, one-story building on Route 431. It's very new, and the decor inside a clash of steel chandeliers and wood paneling. Banks, for all their wealth, reflect only the stark lack of imagination that comes from the constant touch of money. Any human spirit here must have been driven out by the conformity that money imposes on the lives of men. Banks have no poetry, no prose, no songs, no dance. They always remind me of operating rooms—clean, sterile, well lit, and they bare the financial intestines of their customers. A digit here, a zero there, cleanly incised by the razor-sharp computers and adding machines. Only white people are to be seen behind the counters and in the offices.

While I wait 'for Arthur, I flick through a couple of yearbooks lying on the table. The one of Eufaula High has the photographs of both black and white at work, at play, debating, acting. The other yearbook is of a private school, and the children are all white. It is impossible to be objective about the photographs; especially those of the white children in their school play dressed as Ku Klux Klansmen or else boot-polished and dressed to look like "mammies."

Arthur doesn't look too pleased when he comes out of Mac W. Clark the bank official's office. He'd visited the same man six months ago in May of '78, when he'd made his reconnoitering trip to Eufaula. They'd discussed the possibility of the loan, and Arthur was sure he'd be given one the moment he returned South. He'd also spoken to Mac W. Clark a couple of times long-distance from Boston, and had filled in a loan application form.

"When I was home in May I talked to the guy about financing my house," Arthur says as we get into his car. "And he mentioned the fact that it wasn't necessary for me to be workin' here, till I get everything in motion to get started. I mean to get the house built. Now he says we both has to be workin' here before . . . before he can even consider lendin' us enough money to build the house. And he says my wife has to be workin' also because it's a common-law state and . . . I . . . myself cannot get the loan to build the house. I have to have a co-buyer which would be Alma. I don't see why it's necessary for us both to be workin' to get a house you know. My father's willin' to put up the land as collateral. I was hopin' I could just get the house in my name only. But it don't seem to be workin' out that way."

"You sure he said that to you?"

"Sure. He told me and my dad and mom, when we all came here in May," Arthur says. For the first time I've known him, he looks flustered. "I'll get me a job in no time, I know, but now he says Alma's got to work. But Alma wants to go to business school. So how's she goin' to work and study?"

"You think it's because you're black?"

"Yeah," Arthur says quickly. "He makes me mad. He tells me one thing, then when I get here he tells me a different thing. I pack up everything that I own and I move here, now he tells me he can't . . . he don't even know if he can lend me the money. Now that makes me pretty mad 'cause before he told me there was no problem, you see, and now that he got me down here, he tells me he don't know if he can lend me the money. Now that makes me pretty upset you know . . . but I can handle it."

Arthur turns off Route 431, and heads west. It is only here that I see the new small industries that are coming up around Eufaula. There are half a dozen small industrial estates, shiny as new pennies, glittering in the sun.

Arthur, like me, probably does not understand the science of money. Its study demands a cold and rational intelligence, and an understanding of laws that are as complex and mystifying as those that govern the universe. But one thing I do understand. Money is not as blind and as impartial as justice. One scale is weighed down heavily with prejudice: it favors the rich over the poor, success over failure. And, white over black.

Mac W. Clark is a young, neatly dressed white man wearing heavily rimmed spectacles. He also wears a white shirt and tie, and is a rising young executive. His office, just off the main bank foyer, is small. There is just enough space for his desk, and a visitor's chair.

"The qualifications of obtaining a loan here are the same as someone obtaining a loan in any part of the United States," Mac W. Clark says in a faint Southern accent. "A person's character does not come into whether you make a loan or not. I told Arthur Dean Stanford before he made his move back here that, number one, if he was going to move back here before he could obtain a loan he would have to have a job. Or number two, he could remain in Boston and build a house in Eufaula, but if he did that the maximum loan would be eighty percent of the value. It is my understanding that his father would give him enough land to put up this house, and that would qualify the loan on an eighty percent devaluation. Sure I wanted to offer them a move back here but it's hard to remember all the things we talked about, because Arthur Dean came in here very briefly with his mother and father."

The explanation is logical, balanced, fair. It even hints of justice. The laws of the land have been applied impartially, and Arthur has been found wanting. Yet, I have a sense of unease in the face of all this. Laws and rules can, not exactly be waivered, but applied leniently.

"You see Arthur Dean is a little bit different than a lot of people who have come back South," Mac W. Clark continues. "Your . . . er . . . general family coming back home . . . so to speak has had a home or has stayed for a longer period of time in the North. Consequently they have a house, sizable equity generally, and they're coming back home with absolute money. Arthur Dean doesn't have that equity. The fact that his father has land is fine for a down payment, but the amount of the loan he wants is still the same. Even when he gets a job, his wife will have to work as well; and that's not uncommon, white or black. I would say Arthur Dean made a couple of mistakes in obtaining a loan. The biggest one is going through a second party . . . yes . . . his parents. I only talked to him once before he moved here, and the rest of the time it was either through his parents or by correspondence or maybe a phone call. The second mistake that he made was that where Arthur Dean worked in

Boston, with the money he was making, he would have qualified for a loan here. He could've built the house in Eufaula first, and then moved back to his new house. Now when he gets a job here he'll take a drop in income, and that's the reason his wife has to work as well."

Arthur listens in silence to my recital of Mac W. Clark's explanation. When I finish, he looks at me as if I've harmed him in some way.

"He don't tell me . . . no . . . nothin' about stayin' in Boston," Arthur says shortly. "He knew I'd be takin' a drop in pay, but he said that wasn't gonna make a difference in the loan. Or Alma workin'." He lets the echo of indignation fall into a long silence, before turning to me carefully. "What do you think?"

On my answer, I will be judged. He wants a verbal commitment to his cause, someone to ride point and protect his flanks. It is a difficult moment. I also need some room to maneuver, to stand back to understand him that much better. To meet his enemy, disarmed, and report back to him.

Arthur waits.

Yet, I know, impartiality is like a vacuum: it does not exist in man or nature. We may make believe that we have the ability, like gods, to stand detached from the reporting of events but our vision has been permanently impaired by what we are, what we have been.

"He's bullshitting."

"I thought so," Arthur smiles, relaxes.

The road we are traveling after the visit to the bank winds down through a stand of timber. The lake glitters through the trees. A group of workmen are clearing some of the timber, and for a moment, they pause to watch us pass. The road ends at the lake, and a small two-story modern building nestled well into the woods. It's wrap-around glass and on the first floor we can see a few people lining up for lunch. All are white. By the jetty is a power boat.

Arthur goes into Techtronics to meet the personnel man who promised him a job in the small company. He is a bit vague about the offer, nor can he remember the man's name. In fifteen minutes, he's out again, again looking not too pleased.

"They said they'd let me know," Arthur says as we head back into town. The workmen have also taken their lunch break, and now sit on their machines sipping Cokes and rustling open plastic bags. "I filled in a form, but they didn't have an immediate openin'."

He looks calm and not quite as unsettled as when he emerged from the bank. He is silent for a long time, and I can sense the worry. He has saved money, but not enough to completely stave off panic. Besides, Arthur has always been proud of his ability to work and support his family.

"You going to wait for them to give you a job?"

"They didn't say when. And I can't afford to."

We drive into Eufaula, and past some of the white houses. There is such a sense of peace here, of order. I can imagine that these people wouldn't have to worry like Arthur, scrambling for the pickings of jobs to support his wife and child. Arthur stops in front of the state employment office. It's a low, bunker-type building, built to a bureaucrat's imagination. It is a large hall, divided in two by a wooden counter. The folding chairs for the applicants are empty. Behind the counter are half a dozen white people absorbed in their forms and pens and paper clips.

Arthur gives his social security card to the receptionist, a bespectacled girl, and after a short wait he's led to one of the desks behind the counter. His interviewer is a young man. He pulls out a form from his desk. Name, address, telephone number, previous employment, and then previous to that, addresses, years of experience, pay scales. At the end of the interview, he hints at the prospect of a job in a company called Roller Die, on State Docks Road.

Arthur is to see a Mr. Potoff. If he has no luck there the employment officer will try somewhere else. The money isn't going to be much; in fact, less than what Arthur had expected.

"I'd like to ask one question," Arthur says, as he's about to leave. "I left Eufaula six years ago 'cause there weren't many jobs around here. You think the job situation has changed?"

"A lot's changed," the interviewer says. "I wasn't here when you left, but now a lot of different jobs have opened up. I think the prospects are pretty good, depending on your employer here. Back then it was pretty rough. There's more industry too . . ."

"Even for black people?" Arthur interrupts politely.

"Yes, I think so."

The interviewer gives Arthur the directions to Roller Die, and we leave with the appointment card.

"You going to try it?"

"Yeah. I think I will." We stroll over to the car. "You know that girl who first met me. Yeah, that one. Dot. She knowed me. We went to school together. She sure didn't show it, did she. Eufaula's still awful prejudiced, and they try to hide it but you . . . you can feel it, you know, even though they try to cover it up, I can sense it's still prejudiced here. The black people who've never left Eufaula and have lived here all their lives, they . . . they seem to think it's changed, but I think if they go away to another place and see how life is there and come back and compare it with the life they have here, they'll see it hasn't changed much you know."

Roller Die is a large, long factory building, next to a firm called Columbus Metals. Its parking lot has several dozen cars. Behind the building, almost as white as the afternoon sky, is a huge water tank with EUFAULA painted

89

across it. Arthur goes in to see Mr. Potoff. I'm hoping, even though this isn't exactly what he wants, that he'll get the job. It will give him some space to catch his breath. His ambition, where jobs are concerned in Eufaula, is to work for the Alabama Gas Company. It pays the best, but the jobs are scarce and you need to know a "Man" in order to get a job. Arthur doesn't know any "Man." It appears to be a feudal system of employment. Except here, membership qualifications are less subtle. Just white is enough.

"I got the job," Arthur says as he climbs into the car. "I start next week. Evenin' shift. Four to midnight."

"What's it pay?"

"Two seventy five," and the exuberance melts from his voice.

"That's below minimum, isn't it?"

"Yeah. I was makin' near seven an hour in Boston," Arthur says as we head for his home. "I expected to take a drop, but not this big. They say after a month, they'll make it three. I'll work here till I can get somethin' else better." He slouches behind the steering wheel, an elbow stuck out of the window, the breeze ruffling his hair. He changes the tapes on his machine. The music feels good and fills the car. "You know, they got two standards of wages here. One they pay the white man, one for the black. You can get exactly the same job, but they'll pay the white a buck an hour more for it, and there's no way you can tell."

"You got whites working in Roller Die?"

"Yeah. Doin' the same work as the blacks. When I start work I'm gonna check. But they won't tell how much they get paid. Whites stick together you know, Much more than blacks. Everybody talks about the South changin' since desegregation, and they says there's equal opportunities. Nothin'. It was a surprise to me as well. We came home just on visits, and I guess it's because we never went out and met white people on a day-to-day basis. It

90

didn't seem so prejudiced then, and I really thought it had changed. But now we're livin' here, we find it's really there, you know. They're really prejudiced, you know, it's a little like they don't want you to get no place."

"You hurt easily?"

"Yeah, I hurt easy," Arthur says. "My skin . . . it's not too thick . . . but when people do things to me, I don't jump you know. My temper's not so high. I can let things pass, you know, and I don't get violent that easily. Of course, things do make me mad awful easy, but I don't want to fight, and go on like that type of violence. I think things can be solved without fightin' and sheddin' blood, you know. Sit down and talk things over, reason with each other. You can accomplish more that way than with comin' into bodily contact. Like hittin', bleedin', cuttin'. Killin' possibly."

Violence arises out of fear; it is the final act of self-preservation. The white man in the South was constantly haunted by the nightmares of his own making. In a reverse act of colonialism, instead of him going forth to rule the natives of distant countries, he brought them to his own doorstep, and constantly lived in that special kind of fear. The specter of the black man, always in greater number than the white, rising in revolt to destroy his masters, has never loosed its hold on the white imagination. In this context the Southern white was no different from the Roman or the French or the Dutch or the British in their ownership of alien races. Violence was a necessary tool. It was to be used suddenly, erratically, en masse or individually, to hold down the revolts of a subject people; to instill a constant sense of fear equal to or even greater than that experienced by the rulers. The lynchings, the castrations, the tarrings and burnings were no lesser weapons than those used by other similar colonial powers. Revolt. Repression. Revolt. Repression. It is a familiar melody, which never ever stops. It only grows softer at times.

91

He is his father's son. I cannot see Bud turning to violence. I would expect anger, a natural passion, kept under tight control. Bud's veneer of civilization, in the circumstances of their lives, is surprising. I would have expected a sullen and rebellious anger. The last lynching that occurred in Alabama was in the 1950s; nearly a decade after the explosion of the first nuclear device. It's as if the South made a special effort to preserve its own form of feudalism against the sophistication of mass death. I suppose like a poet needing symbolism, to illustrate some profound point, so the lynch mob needed the rope to remind themselves that they could kill a man in the most frightening manner possible. The pistol, the shotgun, the bludgeon, even a laser beam would have robbed the act of the 'romance.'

"Do you think you can sit down and talk to white people?"

Arthur Dean considers. "Well, you could probably. But I don't think it would do any good, because of the fact that they'll sit down and talk with you, but they'll talk around and it ends up so you don't get no place, you know. So you'd only be wastin' time. It's goin' to take more than patience, I think, because the odds are stacked against me. To sit down and talk, I think, it'll take a lot of lookin' to find the right person. Maybe they'll talk to you and maybe they'll talk in your favor when they are before your face, but when they get behind your back it'll be a different story, you know."

The house has returned to life. The children are out in the yard, the chicken population appears to have increased, Bud is tinkering with his car, and Alma is sitting out on the swing. Arthur reports the day's mixed news. Bud listens calmly. Alma does not. She and Arthur take a long walk to the front gate and spend some time, heads together, discussing their problems.

"Well. It's not exactly what he wanted," Bud says from under the hood of the car, "but he's got to have patience.

Nothin' happens right away, does it? He can do this job awhile, until he finds himself a better one. That is bad news about the house, but that's goin' to take time as well."

There's been an addition to the household. Denise, Arthur's young sister, has returned for the weekend from Montgomery. She is eighteen, slim and very pretty. She resembles Arthur, the same delicacy, the well-defined contours of a face with high cheekbones, and bright golden eyes. She is at junior college in Montgomery, and returns home every weekend. Either a friend brings her, or else Bud drives up to collect her. There's a marvelous feeling of innocence about her, a pleasure at being alive. She is alert, intelligent, insatiably curious.

"I've never been anywhere, besides Montgomery," she wrinkles her nose at her own restrictions. She speaks quickly, bubbling, with that Alabaman drawl hurried beyond its own leisurely pace. "I'll tell you what I want to do when I finish school. I got two ambitions," she considers them seriously, and then says: "Either I want to work in television . . . you know . . . behind the camera. Or I think I'll become an actress. I think I want to be an acress more."

"That means you'll have to leave Eufaula?"

"I'd never leave here. Not permanently. I love Eufaula too much," she says. "I'd go and always come back. Yeah, like Arthur Dean does. I'm goin' to come back famous and rich and buy myself a house around here. What do you think I should become. An actress, or television . . . producer?"

"I'd suggest a producer," I say. "It isn't as glamorous, but it has a much longer 'life.' You can keep doing it as long as you can."

"What would I need for that?" Denise asks, her head tilted to the side, studying me. "Like I'm studyin' secretarial stuff now. Should I keep doin' that or should I join a producers' school?"

"There's no producer's school, but you could do courses in communications and the media. But whatever you do, you have to start from the bottom . . . as an errand girl or typist. Then they work you up."

She considers me gravely and sits back. "What would you do?"

"I'd do your secretarial course, as you're already studying it. Finish and then apply to a college that does communications courses. But some of the stations prefer people with a general arts degree."

"But there's no excitement in it is there," Denise says, her face lighting up. "You don't get in front of the cameras." She tosses her head. "Millions don't get to see you."

"No."

"That's what I want to do then," she says firmly. "I want to be like Cecily Tyson or someone like that. Where everyone loves me, and recognizes me."

"It's a very tough profession."

"That depends, doesn't it," and she shrugs off the struggle lightly. "I suppose I'll have to go to Hollywood. Or would New York be better. What should I do?"

"Hollywood is for movies and television. New York is for the stage. Which one do you want?"

"Oh television," she bursts out. "I could be on one of those shows. The Jacksons." She preens prettily, and with a sense of humor. Chuckling to herself at the coming fame.

"In that case, you've got to go to Los Angeles."

"Oh I don't mind that. Then what?"

"Let's see," she waits quietly as I try to remember how the famous stars began their careers. "You'll have to enroll in an acting school, and get yourself an agent to handle you, and go to millions of auditions."

"That sounds simple," she says and falls silent. Her thoughts are miles away, already in Hollywood and on the television screen in millions of homes.

94

"It's tough. A lot of people try; most never make it."

"Oh I will," she says confidently. "Does Boston have television?"

"Yes, but they don't use too many actors or actresses there."

"And New York?" she asks again.

"That's stage."

She wrinkles her nose at that. In Eufaula the stage isn't a familiar medium, even films are rare in that one movie house. Only television dominates her consciousness.

"I guess it will just have to be Los Angeles," she says with a funny resignation.

"What'll your parents think about that?"

"Oh they won't want me to leave," Denise says, at first sadly, and then she brightens. "But when I get famous and come back that'll make them happy."

Arthur and Alma have returned from their walk. Alma sits on the swing, her feet on the ground to keep it from moving. Arthur stands on the porch with his arms folded, staring into the distance.

"Well I'll be looking for you on television then?"

"What's that?" Alma asks.

"I'm going to be an actress," Denise says, standing up, "and we were just discussin' it."

"You should do whatever you want to do," Alma says. "And don't let anyone talk you out of it."

Denise skips into the house to help her mother in the kitchen. Alma looks at Arthur. They both appear fractionally smaller to my eyes, as if something has been taken from them.

"What do you think?" Alma asks me.

"It's not much money he's going to get," I say.

"Not much?" she echoes, glancing at me and tossing her head. Though the action has become familiar she has a surprising command of many subtleties to that gesture. This time it is a sarcastic understatement. "He may as well pick cotton. We can't live on that money. And how we

95

goin' to get money for the house? How am I goin' to study? I'm not goin' to sit around just working . . ." She falls silent after the outburst. The only sound is of Bud's spanner; metallic and hostile to their mood.

Odie comes out of the house with Keith clinging to her skirt. For a moment the three remain on the porch together, then Alma goes in, and Arthur strolls over to join his father.

"He's got to have patience," Odie says. Bud echoes. "I always say things will work out for those who wait."

The Chauncey Sparks State Technical College, named after an ex-governor of Alabama, sits well back from Highway 431. Across the road from it is part of Lake Eufaula. The college is a modern two-story building with little character, too obviously an educational institute. Inside, it smells of classrooms and chalk dust, and that peculiar stale smell of bodies crowded together.

Alma glances up at the portraits of Alabaman governors, grimaces at Wallace, and follows the directions to the office. In a classroom by the entrance half a dozen students, black and white, are learning hair dressing. The school is only for certain skills. Business courses for typing and simple bookkeeping, car repair, masonry, building, radio and television repairing.

"My cousin studied TV repairin'," Arthur says after studying their pamphlet. "He did it three years ago, and still doesn't have a job."

"What's that mean?"

"Nobody'll hire him," Arthur says. "He's gone back to fixin' cars. I was goin' to do somethin' like he did, but now I figure I won't."

It's Alma's turn now to collect the forms, and answer questions, and collect more forms, and answer even more questions. No life can ever be a secret. These papers are the confessionals of society. They do not want the lurid flesh of our lives; they gouge deeper to the truths of how we have constructed ourselves. They listen, make no judgments, but can, if the pen should slip, deliver a terrible retribution. It is there under the "signature." The truth only is required, and the penalties for lying are a sort of bureaucratic damnation.

I would have expected these offices to have a few black women behind those high, electric typewriters. Those courses for business administration, typing, accounting could surely have trained enough to have filled at least these positions. But there are none, and I wonder in which wilderness they have been consigned with those skills.

Alma has to be interviewed by a course instructor. He is young, white, impeccably neat with a very complicated clock sitting behind him on a file cabinet. It tells the time by the rolling, on different planes, of ballbearings, and every five minutes there is a terrible clatter of these steel balls falling, rolling and returning to their level. I am amused by these unnecessary advances in technology.

Rob, as he wants to be called, is friendly and polite. He outlines the courses she can take: secretarial science, general clerical, bookkeeping and accounting. Alma picks the most complete one.

"Why?" he asks.

"Because I think maybe me and my husband can go into some business of our own. Then we could keep our own books and stuff." She gives me a you-don't-know-everything-about-me look and returns to the interview.

Alma is relentless in her interest to discover what all these qualifications will finally benefit her. How much will she earn? Raises? How much travel? His answers are an obvious disappointment. After a year of study, Alma will only begin at the minimum wage level. Two sixty-five an hour.

"Possibly three," Rob demurs. It fails to move Alma.

"Is that what *everybody* starts at?" Alma asks.

"It depends on the company."

"Depends!" Alma mutters as we all go back to Arthur's car. She clutches her pamphlets tightly. She has promised the man to enroll at the start of the next semester, and she's going to fill out yet another form for federal assistance. "What's that mean?" she asks indignantly. "Depends on your color . . . if they ever get round to hiring you after you spend all that money and time."

"You're goin' to get a job aren't you?" Arthur asks.

"'Course I am. I'll work evenings."

"But after all that studying how are you going to get a really good job?" I ask.

"I think you have to sell yourself," Alma says, sitting back in the seat. "If I go into some place and just let them give me that two sixty-five an hour . . . the two ninety . . . whatever, and I've spent a year and a half in college and got an associate's degree I think that would be my stupidity to go in and take that two-ninety-an-hour job. I feel that way about all the black people here that went to college and go take a lower paying job when they know they're qualified for something better. So I wouldn't take the job. If I'm good which I know I hope I will be, and if I'm good at business, the typing and bookkeeping that I'm gonna take, I think I can find a job and I can set my own price. It all depends on how good I am and how good I do in school."

Arthur glances at her: affection, confidence. "She won't have trouble findin' a job," he says.

"I never expected it to be easy," Alma says. "We gave up one kind of life for another. Starting again. It's going to take time . . . to adjust."

I sense it's going to take more than time; it's going to take a reversal in her mentality. She isn't supposed to be confident, so uppity in Alabama. She will also have to lessen her ambitions, accept the two sixty-five or two ninety. When there's a pool of cheap labor, it's always a buyer's market.

"You disco?" Alma suddenly turns and asks.

"Sure."

"Then you going to hit the high spot in downtown Eufaula tonight."

T.J.'s isn't hard to find at ten at night. There is no sign on the door, no swirling lights, and only the faintest whisper, not even that, more a feel through the walls and the sidewalk, of hidden music. It is also the only doorway with any sign of activity on Broad Street. The building itself looks like one of those familiar western hotels. A long porch supported by slender columns covers most of the sidewalk. T.J.'s is also the only disco within a radius of twenty miles.

Alma is dressed in a pretty, silkish dress, revealing bare shoulders and an expanse of back. Arthur is wearing a fawn suit with a vest, and no tie. They are, I discover, overdressed for T.J.'s. They are the city slickers in the small-town disco.

It costs two bucks to get in, and the pretty blond woman at the door stamps the back of our hands with fluorescent ink. The blond appears friendly with some of the black men who are standing just inside the door. She is the only white woman in T.J.'s. Behind the bar, serving the drinks, is the only white man. The disco isn't particularly large, but it is particularly dark because of the deep brown stucco ceiling, which has a few holes in it, and in some places looks as if it is about to fall down. At the far end, in front of the turntables and giant speakers, is the dance floor. It is raised a couple of feet off the bar floor, and we watch the dancers from a table by the door and within convenient reach of the bar.

The dancers are ceaseless. There is nothing stylized or formal about their movements; each is individualistic and expressive. They translate the music, its subtlest rhythms, with such ease. Between the sound and this visual pattern of arms and legs and torso there seems to be little distance. They are one and the same.

"Come and dance," Alma orders me.

It's been some time, too much time, since I've been on a disco floor. And that was quite a distance from T.J.'s, and where the other dancers were as awkward as I was. I could excel among those mediocrities, sweating to the surface sound of the music and giving no heart to its deeper rhythms, but here, amidst all this grace, I feel a child being coaxed onto a stage.

"You can't!" Alma mocks. Arthur laughs. "Come on. I'll teach you." They are both taking delight at my embarrassment.

"It's too late for that." And it's also too late to grab another shot of scotch at seventy-five cents.

Alma and Arthur have me out of the seat and are pulling and pushing me to the dance floor. The music should envelop me as it does the "real" dancers, but it only batters against my ears as we push our way through the crowd. The odds, I notice, of men to women is around ten to one, and here, far from the door, is the distant sweet odor of marijuana.

Alma is a beautiful dancer. She blends, graceful and sensual, to the music. I catch glimpses, between the sudden bursts of the strobe light, her grinning at me. I can only heavily imitate the men and women around me. I can remember, years ago, an African friend trying also to teach me how to dance. He was a patient, instructive man. A foot here, a foot there, the arms this way, the knees bent. I envied his ease, and failed him. Dance is innate; it travels with the soul.

Agnes and her husband have joined the table when Alma and I return. Arthur's older sister looks a plumper version of Denise, and she is as friendly as her mother. She lives with her husband and two children in Eufaula. He is a big heavy-boned man who works in a lumber yard.

Alma and Arthur dance well together. It is obviously a familiar part of their lives. In Boston, they went to a disco two or three times a week, and a different one each time. When the music turns romantic, they dance closer, Alma resting her head on his shoulder. They talk quietly, whispering and smiling at each other. Too soon the mood is broken for them and they return to the table.

By midnight, there's hardly room to move. The number of whites, however, hasn't increased.

"Where do they go?" I ask.

Arthur shrugs. I could well have asked him where reindeer go in spring.

"I think to that place I showed you. You know, outside Eufaula," he says. "This used to be their disco, and then the blacks began comin' and took it over."

The whites and blacks in this town are strangers to each other. Their lives only brush against each other infrequently. Physically and economically, they must touch and spring apart, and if the white doesn't "see" the black man, it is equally true that the black man does not "see" the white. They occupy parallel spaces, like science fiction characters in a world where the laws of the universe become magical. They seem studiedly unaware of the other's physical presence. Submerged in the lives of Arthur and Alma and the family and friends and relatives, I'm aware that I too have not "seen" the white. Their presence has been noted but at a great and unreachable distance.

CHAPTER 9

Mansions of the Mind

André Malraux once commented that a museum is a comparatively recent invention, and that it imposes an artificial attitude on the part of the spectator. The objects we examine in a museum were originally conceived as everyday artifacts, and it is we who elevate them to "works of art." The Shorter Mansion in Eufaula does not preserve works of art; it entombs a memory. We are asked to imagine that once we cross its threshhold we have entered the past. It is not a Tara, nor is it accurately antebellum. Its graceful sixteen columns, and the elegant air of plantation magnificence, are scaled-down imitations of what a Tara might have been. Although most of the Shorter Mansion was built in 1906, the central part of the structure was a house that existed in the mid-19th century.

The Mansion is well kept. Its custodians are the genteel ladies who live in the other mansions of the town. They have taken pains to ensure that each visitor becomes aware of all the furnishings in the building. There is a French Empire chandelier in the entry hall, an Empire chest, with heavy acanthus-leaf carving in the center hall. The draperies in the double parlors were donated by Kirvens Department store in Columbus, Georgia. There are paintings of Indians and Italian Urns and a Rosewood Square Grand piano. The framed invoice for the piano is dated 1869, and the price was four hundred and fifty dollars. There is a framed sheet of music, "The Eufaula Waltz," that was composed by a Polish composer, and dedicated to a Miss Carrie Caruthers, in 1850. There are portraits of six governors from Barbour County, and a photograph of Earth taken by Apollo 8. As I walk through more rooms I am reminded of a visit I made to a Maharajah's palace. It smelled damp, the walls were cracked, the paintings of princes were mildewed, ancient swords rusted on walls, tapestries were torn by age, and my footsteps echoed down long marbled corridors. That palace became a symbol for the past dying. But in the Shorter Museum, history has been scavenged and the pieces bolted together with little sense of continuity. Eras leap and clash, one against the other, and when they fall, they leave us no key to why it has been preserved. The pamphlets and booklets give only the details of the white mansions in Eufaula. They explain nothing about the people who live behind those walls. One of the caretakers says she knows someone who can tell me about white Eufaula.

Lucien Abraham is a tall, spare man with intelligent eyes. He lives in a white gothic house not far from the Shorter Mansion. His library with its deep, comfortable armchairs and a fireplace, overflows with books. Abraham is an insurance agent by profession with a hunger for learning.

"I'm not quite the local historian," Abraham says, "but more the local eccentric."

Abraham first came to Eufaula in the winter of 1956. He grew up in a small town in Arkansas, on the banks of a river in the Ozark Mountains. "I fell in love with the place when I first came here," he says. "And so did my family. Eufaula was a clearly defined community and somewhat unique. But it was not a uniqueness that I didn't expect to find. The part of Arkansas I come from is similar to this part of Alabama. What you find in a community like this is a gentle, very satisfying and open atmosphere. You're not accepted immediately as a member of the community, but you're welcomed into the community. The people, because of their history, tend to be rather well educated and rather articulate and conscious of their history."

In spite of twenty-three years of residence, Abraham still doesn't consider himself a native Eufaulian.

"Well, I think there are three things that have contributed to the character of the people here and to the community," Abraham says. "To my mind, and one is not more important than the other, but the first one that comes to mind is the Civil War itself. The Civil War was much more than a fight over whether Alabama should be a slave state or not. It involved the very soul of the people who lived here at the time. It had to do with States' Rights. Should we have a government in Washington so strong that it could tell us what to do, or should we be complete masters of our own fate? Also the federal government had a good deal to say about foreign trade, and the big crops in the South were produced for foreign trade. Whereas in the Yankee part in the North they were producing manufactured goods for their own consumption. So the Civil War was important; and it was a lost cause and as people often do, we tend to embrace lost causes. So we embraced that part of our history that seemed most glamorous. Where chivalry was in full flower and gentle country life was the dream of every person. We are still embracing that relatively short period of time when there was great wealth and when the social life in Eufaula was very active. It was not uncommon for Shakespearian troups to come through and Efloree [an arts festival] was the most important social event and lasted for several days. So that makes us a community that forgets about all the bad things of plantation life, and makes us tend to remember the glamor."

This memory of glory is unnaturally long. And unhealthy. Glory should remain firmly buried in the past. It cannot be transported from its moment in time for it fades and tarnishes. It should remain as a memory, and never as a living presence for it can distort the past as well as one's vision of the present.

"Another very important part of the South is that there are two communities here, the black and the white communities, but beyond that there's not anything else," Abraham continues. "If the ten to twelve thousand people who live in Eufaula now were to live in a two- to three-block area of New York City, let's say, on the one side there might be a group of Greeks, on the other side Italians, and somewhere down the street a group of Hispanic people. You just don't find that anywhere in the South. Harry Golden says this is the biggest backyard in America. Every community is so much the same. There are a few Germans, there is always the small Jewish community of merchants in any little town in the South, and there's the black community and the white community. There is just very little exposure to something else. We're almost totally without contacts with any Asiatic people, with any of the huge Polish block from Europe. So we don't know anything about them. A person like me with the name Abraham will move into a community like this and have a little bit of a problem because Abraham is not English or Scottish or Irish."

I wonder aloud if this prejudice is really a fear of the unknown.

"Well, prejudice is always a function of one's education or ignorance, is it not?" Abraham says. "And so you find prejudice expressed in the South just the way you would expect it. We would be prejudiced against those things that we're not familiar with, and we would be prejudiced against those things that perhaps we're too close to. A great deal of bitterness was created immediately after the Civil War during Reconstruction when the radical Congress took away the voting privileges from the white Southerner and gave it to the black Southerner. But even to say this prejudice was caused by that is an oversimplification. The blacks were . . ." he hesitates a moment, ". . . servants and they were generally, a good many of them at least, liked and respected. This prejudice is aimed not so much at the blacks themselves, but it's aimed at the terrible decision one has to make when he is forced by some outside force to change his way of thinking, his way of living. If one has always lived in a white neighborhood, and if all of the neighbors had the same names as you—Johnsons, Barnets, Smiths, and McKays—and then you're faced with the prospect that blacks might move in the same neighborhood, it's frightening.

"And the prejudice in the South goes further than that in that since we have not been exposed to people from a broad range of ethnic backgrounds. We're just ignorant of those and we tend to distrust them. We're all so much the same. It's good in that it makes each community comfortable with itself, but its bad in that it makes you narrow as you grow."

Jean Renoir once made the comment that the problems of the world stemmed from the fact that "every man has a reason." Lucien Abraham presents me with reasons, and I think I understand them. With variations, I have found such reasons in Indian villages, English towns, generously scattered through all the communities of men. Prejudices are the dark mantles covering our insecurities, they lie in layers, like ancient circles of fortifications, not so much protecting the mind, but the heart. They are "reasonable" nightmares which cannot be exorcised by learning.

"And then there's the third thing," Abraham says. "I'm not sure how I can put this so that it's accurate. I don't want to talk down about this, but it's religion. Religion is a terribly . . . terribly strong force here. We are heirs to the puritan Protestant ethic that came with the first waves of people through this part of the country. The Roman Catholics are a very small minority here. This is largely Baptist and Methodist and Presbyterian. So the Protestant work ethic—work as hard as you can, make all you can make, save as much as you can save, and give some of that to the church—is a part of our body and souls here; and that fierce independence that marked earlier America is best expressed through Southern Baptists. That's what you find most everywhere. It is interesting to me that in the churches of the South that are not connectional—that is, such as the Baptist church that has no hierarchy connecting the church in Eufaula, for example, with the church in Birmingham—there is a tendency among those church congregations to reinforce the prejudices and the feelings of each community. Whereas in the much smaller representations in the Episcopal and Presbyterian churches there is a little bit of an outside influence on these congregations. So you don't tend to get your prejudices quite as reinforced in those churches as you do in Southern Baptist. I know that sounds terribly critical, and I don't mean it that way at all, but it is a fact of life in those churches. So the local preacher and the religious community is part of the fabric of life, and you can't separate it as you could perhaps in some other part of the United States."

There are Catholic and Protestant churches in Eufaula. This number does not include the small black churches scattered around the countryside. Abraham is a Pres-

107

byterian. The Stanfords are Methodist. I've no doubt of religion's importance. On Sundays, the television turns into a pulpit.

The earliest settlers into this part of Alabama were the French and a few Scots. There were also the Spanish who'd built a fort about thirty miles north up stream from Eufaula on the banks of the Chattahoochi River and occupied it from 1689 to 1691. They were gradually driven out by English settlers coming in from Georgia who founded the large plantations and raised rice, indigo, tobacco, and later, cotton.

"The large landowners that came then really left their mark here," Abraham says. "They were ambitious, talented, hardworking, avaricious people. They came with the idea of Empire. And that always leads to the controversy of States' Rights. 'I shall grow my Empire here and no one shall tell me what to do.'

"I was told as a young man in school that they came seeking freedom, but I don't believe that. They came seeking to set up the same sort of tyranny they'd just escaped from in Europe. Only this time they were going to be the tyrants, instead of the tyrannized. These people were so influential that they still affect our way of thinking down here. Much of the political leadership of the United States prior to the Civil War came from that group of people. There were poets, writers, a great deal of culture . . ."

The North, according to Southern mythology, could not compete. They did not have the time nor the leisure to write sonnets to lovely ladies, music for the balls, read those European writers, develop a Southern charm and gallantry. The situation in the South was that with such a huge pool of slave labor, the Southerner had greater advantages in developing the cultural side of life. He was given those advantages—time and leisure—by the slaves he owned.

I ask him when this way of life began to really change.

"I think World War II was an enormously important social event even though the war was fought thousands of miles away. Had it not been for that war, there would be a great many people in this country who would have lived out their lives and not got a hundred miles from home. They would never have been exposed to the countries they were exposed to. They would never have found out that people with different accents had pretty much the same fears and values. Prior to World War II this was a very settled community. I'm not that familiar with European history but I would have thought we would have been very European here. If you were a landowner you were part of the nobility; if you were a merchant you were a part of the merchant class; if you were a workman, you were a workman. All the families reflected this structure and there wasn't much change. A workman didn't become a merchant and a merchant didn't become a landowner, and the blacks had their place, we like to say, and stayed in it.

"During all those years it didn't occur to black families that there might be something better, some way they could improve themselves. The black leaders who came along after World War II and before the desegregation act of 1954 were the first people who articulated hopes that must have been dormant for a long time. You can do other things, you can own your own home, you can go live in a nice neighborhood, you can walk the streets without fear. When that began to penetrate their consciousness, they became restless. They wanted a part of the greater American Dream. The blacks who served in World War II saw for the first time what this country was like. Those who'd never been outside Barbour County perhaps sat down in a restaurant right next to a white man some place up North. It would have been a heady experience, terrifying I suspect. Before World War II there was no possibility of change here, because this was the best of all possible worlds. You really didn't need very much money and the most charming and delightful generation of women ever produced in any part of the United States, to my mind, grew up here. They couldn't cook, but they were marvelous hostesses, great conversationalists, delightful people. I can remember a lady in her eighties, who's since died, who was one of the most beautiful women I've ever seen. She was a product of that lifestyle. And then the desegregation decision came along and threatened to change that beautiful, well-settled, well-understood, loved lifestyle."

He pours a drink. Evening has come. The lights go on. The return of his wife is signaled by the entry of an ancient boxer. His wife is a pretty, charming woman; the daughter who follows her in, beautiful. They are soft and graceful. Abraham's words echo: "They couldn't cook, but they were marvelous hostesses, great conversationalists, delightful people." It takes little to imagine both in that other era, that time of innocence.

On the following day Abraham takes me to a cotton plantation. The sun is hot. The dust is following the large green machine that moves slowly down the rows of cotton bushes, and it hangs like a pall of red smoke over the immediate landscape. In every direction as far as I can see, are rows of green bushes flecked white with cotton.

Lucien Abraham talks with the wife of the plantation owner, while I try to imagine what it felt like for Alma to pick cotton. Sweat stings my eyes, the shirt sticks to my back, dust quickly dries on the sweat. It's hard to part the cotton bud from the plant; you need to twist it savagely. The ground between the rows is hard, uneven, and the bushes scrape against my bare arms and catch at my jeans. When I look up, the row appears to reach the horizon.

The cotton picking machine, driven by a black man perched high above the twisting spikes that bore into the cotton and pluck it and have the fluffs blown back into the cage behind, reaches the end of a row, turns and starts back again. It is, I'm told, a very expensive machine.

"We can't get folks no more to pick the cotton," the lady tells me. She is embarrassed by my presence. She doesn't want her name mentioned, nor the name of the plantation. The ownership of a cotton plantation obviously evokes the wrong memories. She is self-conscious: it's as if she owned a galley which is now driven by deisel engines, but the benches and chains remain. In some ways they do. The long driveway leading to the plantation house is red dirt, and it passes by black children sitting in the dust, outdoor hand pumps, and mean shanties. There is no glass to the windows. Sagging doors guard the privacy of the families.

Not fifty yards away, is the plantation owner's residence. It's a large white building, not as picturesquely antebellum as I'd expected, but still generous in its proportions. The architecture is partially Gothic. Inside, it is expensively furnished and complete with a bar room, a dining room with cabinets filled with bone china, and photographs in the recreation room, dominated by an electronic organ, of young white couples dressed in tuxedos and ball gowns.

After the walk in the cotton fields I visit the gin. The air is full of fine white fibers that cling to my hair and clothes, and tickle the insides of my nostrils. An old white man supervises the work of a dozen black men unloading the cotton from the trailers, cleaning it, and packing the compressed bales that emerge from the other end of this noisy, wheezing machine. The men have indigo skins, streaked white with cotton and age. They say little to each other as they work, there is no apparent camaraderie. It could be because the owner is with me. But the machine does not allow for comfort. It has to be constantly fed with freshly plucked cotton, and at the other end, the bales have to be loaded. I detach myself from my companions, and wander through the gin. An old black man watches me. His teeth have decayed.

"How long have you been working here?"

"All my life," he says. "I been doin' this every day, yassuh. I live up on the estate. There ain't no other work around, yassuh."

The machine recalls him to his constant labor. It's hot, the air almost unbreathable. The sun after the darkness of the shed is brilliant, blinding.

"Desegregation has produced some interesting results to my mind here," Abraham says, as we return to Eufaula. "The first reaction all of us had to desegregation was fear and anger. We recognized, I think, within our hearts even if we didn't say it publicly long before that, that the blacks were being mistreated. We were aware that we had to make some redress in our political operations. We had schools for blacks, we knew they were inferior, but it was the way things were done and since we were such a community of sameness all over the South it never occurred to us to change. Some of that change had taken place though, prior to the landmark Civil Rights decision in 1954. It was spotted, it was very small. But here in Eufaula none of that change had taken place at all; tradition is so important here. There were black schools and there were white schools, and the black schools were very inferior to the white schools. They were separate but certainly not equal. So in '54, the first reaction was fear. 'Good heavens, my child might have to sit down right next to a black boy or girl.' The anger: 'My children shall not be forced to go to a black school that's been terribly inferior to the white school.' And then, after a time had elapsed, the latent decency of these people began to come forward, and my observations tell me there was a great deal of genuine progress along the main streets and thoroughfares and small towns in the South. The animosity began to drop away. There is a genuine feeling of closeness to the blacks that's beginning to rise again.

"Now the blacks are a threat to white jobs. And that

stops their progress. If you're an old landowning family in Alabama and you're secure economically you don't feel that pressure much. But if you're a blue-collar worker in one of the industries in town here, and your job is threatened by the rise of the black people, then you feel that threat. So now, strangely enough in the Old South where the largest population of blacks are—across this belt of Alabama—the animosity towards them is slowly diminishing. Whereas in the northern part of Alabama, where there is a much larger blue-collar community, there is much more desolation, the animosity continues to be very strong. It is an interesting paradox as there are not that many blacks in northern Alabama as there are in the South. Until very recently, there are signs I have seen across certain county lines in north Alabama, with big letters painted on them: 'Nigger don't let the sun sit on your head in this county.' You never saw that kind of thing here in the very cradle of the black belt."

"Do you know the Stanford family?" I ask.

"Not personally, but since meeting you I made some inquiries about them," Abraham says. "They are a well-respected family in Eufaula, and quite well known. I think with the young Stanfords' first move back here they'll find large gaps in the American Dream. One of the most important gaps, and it may not seem so at first glance, is recreation. If you have a black skin and live in Eufaula, Alabama or in Barbour County, you have a good job, you have a hundred dollars in your pocket, your wife's in good clothes, and you're in good clothes and you want to spend a night on the town, where would you go? What would you do? If you want to take a young child to a nice clean chlorinated swimming pool, where would you find one? There isn't one. If you want to play golf, there's just now opening up a public golf course. We whites tend to take so much for granted, but it's difficult for black families to find ways to spend their time.

"The other thing is the availability of jobs. Now there's

been a great deal of progress made here, more jobs are available for black people here than there has been ever before. The problem for these black people is getting the better-paid jobs. That's coming very slowly and very inequitably, but it's coming. My feeling is that the more jobs that are available the more money blacks have to spend. And the more they'll have to clean up their act, so to speak, so that they don't come to restaurants as filthy workmen as they once did, and as whites still do to some degree.

"Now I think the Stanfords will find great frustration, some opportunities, a great many changes they like and they'll find an enormous need to express themselves in ways that they'll find very difficult now. The American Dream for everyone is still hard to come by in the South, but it is a possibility now for the Stanfords. A generation ago it was an impossibility."

Lucien Abraham has a small, light-filled study at the rear of his house. There are windows on all sides of the small room, and it looks out on his back garden. A large, bushy-tailed squirrel scampers up and down a tree like an absentminded traveler.

"I will try to explain," Abraham says. "There's in Eufaula now a kind of difficult conflict going on in a number of people's minds. There are young people who are finding it possible to have a good friend that is black. It is possible for a black child to come into the yard next door to play touch football with the white boys that live there. They enjoy that and the parents look at that and say 'Gosh, that's good for my children.' But when you're faced with something else: how far will that contact go? That is: how far am I comfortable with social contacts with blacks? We all have to admit there are certain barriers we raise, certain areas beyond which we don't want to go. No one would like to admit that though he would be happy to receive someone at his door, he would not be happy for that same person to sit down to supper with him. I'm lucky enough to have had a background that makes it easier to admit to my own shortcomings I guess, and be a little detached from myself. Maybe that's what makes it easier for me."

Lucien Abraham, I realize, is a permanent outsider in Eufaulian society. He may mix graciously with them, but he's certainly not a member of the elite—the Claytons, the Flewellens, the Kendalls, the McDowells, the Merrels. These are all the old ladies of Eufaula, the committee members who run the annual pilgrimage back to that lost past, and are the final arbitrators of social acceptance. They are in their seventies and eighties and determined to keep the white mansion intact and to pass it from generation to generation, accumulating a confusion of memorabilia. They are unreachable; they remain behind a veil.

"What these changes will be no one can guess, but whatever they are, they have to be bad. And that's the beginning of the problems." Abraham stops, not wanting to continue. "I really think . . . well . . . I shouldn't get into that. I think the federal government made some mistakes by forcing cosmetic changes when being slower and more logical would have made deeper progress."

"What do you mean 'cosmetic changes'?"

"Cosmetic changes are when the federal government sets guidelines that say you have to have so many blacks in so many positions. Then the people who do the hiring, do it with great animosity towards the whole system, and they do it with great animosity towards the people they've hired for those jobs. But when it's done from a different angle, and they are hired because of their merit, then the change is permanent, and it spreads its effects to the people around them."

"I feel it was necessary for the federal government to impose a quota. Otherwise the black would never be given an equal opportunity."

"I don't think so," Lucien says. "A black who has

115

received a job because he's part of a quota doesn't have the same respect that a black who has got his job through his ability and against great odds. I would say one last thing about the Southern mentality. I think we've always felt we're fighting against great odds and that we have respect for people who fight against great odds, so that those people who climb up by their own guts are respected." He sits, removes his spectacles. "So that's the problem that exists now. There are certain things being done because of the federal government saying we have to do them; there are other things being done because people want to do them. That's the difference between a cosmetic change and a change that is permanent and all for the good."

The Eufaula Country Club's golf course, on Country Club Road, undulates gently and comfortably across a road, through stands of pine and disappears over a dip in the land. The grass is very green; the putting circles immaculately shaved. It is a clear, warm afternoon. A lawn mower, driven by a black man in continuously decreasing circles over the second green, across a small vale from the first, faintly, even soothingly, harmonizes with the silence. An electric golf cart, transporting two white gentlemen, hums down into the vale in pursuit of a golf ball. The clubhouse, only a hundred yards from the first green, looks empty. It is a neat, brick, single-story building with a polished oak door. Adjacent to it is a large swimming pool. The water is a pale, blinding blue. A solitary blond woman in a swimsuit and dark glasses reclines on a chair reading a paperback book. The pool and the woman are encircled by a wire fence.

One of the men in the golf car is Ferrel Patrick. The other the Club pro. Patrick is a young, well-tanned, auburn-haired man with a round face. He is the president of the Eufaula Chamber of Commerce. His office is in a little white wood-framed cottage, set in a pretty garden, on Barbour Street, Eufaula. The Patricks are an old Eufaula family, and Ferrel, dressed in a neat blazer, gray slacks, black moccasins and a striped tie, is very wary of any and every question. Soon the large mahogany desk behind which he sits begins to resemble a bunker.

"We in Eufaula are aware of the migration of Northerners to the South. However, we haven't felt the impact quite like the major industrial cities of the South." He has a pleasant Alabaman drawl, the 'ah' instead of the 'I's,' but for him each word looms large as a minefield, and he has to cautiously skirt their potential explosions. "We're not promoting industrial development for the sake of creating jobs. We can be selective. We want to preserve our rich heritage, we're keeping a strong commitment to the preservation of our past and our good quality of life."

"Are you finding it difficult to balance the two?"

He considers carefully: "Well, there's . . . it's a sort of an internal struggle. We've got . . . we've got people who are completely satisfied with the way their life style of the South, the way the . . . the small town Eufaula . . . er . . . the life is completely suitable to their way of thinking. However, we realize that in order not to regress we have to provide jobs."

"How's Eufaula going to cope with the black people who are returning?"

"The people in Eufaula, and I think basically the theory is accurate throughout the South . . . that . . . this . . . there is no ethnic division," Patrick says. "With the exception, possibly, the old black–white relationship. However, there's a strong tradition that . . . in the South . . . there's an old saying and I think it's pretty accurate, 'We don't care how close we get as long as the ethnics don't get too big, and in the North they don't care how big they get as long as they don't get too close.' I think that holds pretty much true with the old South. However, I think the new South is accepting leadership from blacks. It's been a long time since the 1964 Voting Rights Act.

People . . . er . . . the blacks are independent, they vote their own mind, they're not told how to vote. The blacks are being catered to by white politicians. They're a very strong dominant force in our political system, and therefore would be in our economic system. We realize that we all have to work together."

"And possibly live side by side?"

Ferrel Patrick sits back, swings his chair back and forth, as if circling the question.

"Ah . . . as far as the blacks moving into white neighborhoods . . . that is a problem that . . . that we have not faced yet," he finally says. "Ah . . . I don't believe you'll find many areas in the South, especially Eufaula, Alabama, addressing itself to that question. But, it will have to address itself to that question and I believe that . . that we have swallowed some bitter pills in the South." He pauses, flushed, thinly veiling his resentments. "We have accepted court-ordered integration, we have accepted court-ordered improvement in our prison systems and our mental health programs. The Southerners have met these with resistance . . . ah . . . when the resistance broke down we realized this was an inevitable proposition. We adapt to it, and I believe in the South—the Southern people—can adapt to any kind of change. It might take time. We were forced to do things overnight that were extremely difficult. I think the question of migration of blacks into white neighborhoods will be a little slower, and will be an easier proposition to work out. It won't be an overnight proposition. I think that . . . culturally . . . the South has matured. The South is not unlike anywhere else in the country, but I believe that if it becomes inevitable . . . we will realize and recognize the importance of cooperating with our black brothers."

Black brothers! That is a strange remark. It is his effort to redress the balance, to cast himself in a more understanding role. He senses that it sits uneasily in the silence.

"The opportunity for blacks to find very respectable

places in the business community are good," he continues quickly, wanting to erase the word. "We have many black leaders—business leaders and leaders in . . . in the community—that own their own businesses. The most common type of businesses are the trades—the street artisan, the construction trades; we have many brick layers that own their own businesses and do contract work and are very successful at it. We have blacks who are carpenters, many own general stores, grocery stores, laundries, and . . . ah . . . two outstanding funeral home operators, well actually three. And one black is . . . is on the city board of education. So the opportunity for the black man in Eufaula to assume a responsible place in the business community is not bad." He hesitates for a long time. "No . . . there are no black industrialists or bankers . . . and . . . er . . . no members of the chamber of commerce." He returns quickly to the litany of business success for black people. "As a matter of fact we have several Front Street black businesses that at one time . . . the blacks were, the black businesses of the community were relegated to . . . certain areas. However, in the last few years we have seen increasingly blacks take places on very . . . ah . . . prominent locations in town."

The grocery store, the dry goods store, the pawnbrokers, the department stores, the shoe store, the garages, the liquor store, the restaurants, the discotheque, the farm implement store, the supermarket, that are located on the main streets of Eufaula are not owned by blacks. Only one, the supermarket, employs a black cashier. This happened within the last six months. The other stores do employ black errand boys. No black serves a customer.

"I think the types of blacks that would find themselves coming to Eufaula would have to have a keen respect for our heritage," Patrick says. "If they want to hold positions of leadership and positions of responsibility in the

119

community, they will address themselves to the proposition of . . . maintaining and perpetuating our history, our heritage. I feel that if they are willing to make that . . . that sort of commitment to the town, then the town will accept an honest effort on their part. We want to preserve, and we will preserve the heritage, the architecture, the gracious hospitality of our city against any type of invasion. It's a give-and-take situation. I feel if they're going to commit to Eufaula, and they're willing to commit to perpetuating the rich heritage, then the city will commit to them an effort to cooperate."

"If they challenge it?"

"If they challenge, if they choose to challenge our heritage and our . . . ah . . . rich quality of life, the good life, if they challenge the systems of education and government that we've tried hard to perfect, you can be assured they will be met by resistance," Patrick says. It's as if he's become tired of the game he's been playing. "It will be met with resistance anywhere. Any effort to break down a confident and very efficient and very equitable system where one exists, will be met with opposition. And I don't think Eufaula's any different to anywhere else in that respect."

I make a final visit to the Shorter Mansion. Strolling through the rooms, I realize now that, as beauty lies in the eye of the beholder, so memories and history lie in these rooms. Only their eyes can transform this bric-a-brac into something that was once glorious; only their minds can conjure up a two hundred-year-old dream out of a sixty-eight-year-old house.

CHAPTER 10

Old-Time Religion

Freemont Church, the place where the Stanford family worships, lies off a small dirt road. It is about half a mile up from the Stanford home, towards Baker Hill; an old rubber boot, stuck upside down on a stick with its toes pointing towards the church, marks the turn off Route 31.

There is an unfenced graveyard to the left of the dirt road, a few yards before the church. The graves nearest the road are most recent. They have granite headstones. One is marble. Most of the older graves just have wooden crosses. The ground slopes away into the undergrowth and the graves here become anonymous, just dips and bumps in the earth, all well covered by a carpet of decaying leaves. Pecan and oak trees shade this small graveyard from the sun.

"All of my people are buried here," Bud says. A freshly dug grave, with the earth neatly piled to one side, waits for another Stanford.

"My grandmother, grandfather, sister and mother, and

I have a lot of cousins and aunts who are all buried here. I can remember when I was a boy, they used to bring a body out here on a wagon, pulled by mules y'know. They'd get you in, unload it and take it into church and they'd have the funeral. And then they'd bring it out, they'd have five lines to hold the body, and they'd let it down in the grave. They didn't have a box, like they have now. They just let them down in the ground and put a top over, probably a board top and then covered them up with dirt. That was the way my grandmother was buried, and my grandfather, and lot more of my relations was buried like that. Of course my mother, she was buried in a box. She's only been dead about three years now."

The newly dug grave waits for another cousin, Novella Davis. She was in her sixties, and died of a heart attack four days ago. The wake, the funeral services and the burial were delayed so that the Stanford clan could gather. Cousins have come from as far away as California and Texas, Chicago and New York. The California relation has driven for three days with his wife and children in order to attend the service. This funeral is a time not merely for mourning, but for the renewal of ties between the living.

The funeral service by Reverend Alan Lightner is held in the morning. Odie serves a huge lunch in the afternoon, and then later, the burial. There are nearly fifty cars in the procession that start off from the black funeral home in Eufaula, and the small dirt road on this fall afternoon is a contrast of black suits, pretty dresses, and huge arrays of flowers at the graveside. The dust settles on all, pink and light. Novella is buried in an elaborate black casket with brass handles. Her grave will have a marble headstone. The local newspaper, the *Eufaula Tribune*, has printed a short obituary.

"The only time when they write about us," Bud says, "is when we die or when we commit a crime."

Bud is the secretary of the Freemont Church; Odie the

treasurer. Because of the limited resources of the church, a service is held and led by the visiting preacher every alternate Sunday. On those Sundays a preacher doesn't attend, either Bud, Odie, or Denise teach the Sunday-school class.

The church is a simple building. It lies fifty feet off the dirt road, and is raised about three feet above the ground. It is made of wood and the white paint is faded. It is really a hall with a steeple attached to the roof in front. The cross on top is of unpainted wood. The windows are of clear glass. Inside there are a dozen rows of wooden benches on either side of the aisle, and the pulpit is a wooden stand. Behind the pulpit are three rows of benches for the choir. Odie and Alma and Denise sing in the choir. Next to them is an upright piano. The only decoration is a framed picture of Christ and a religious calendar. At the rear is a small changing room. It is furnished with a table and a chair.

"I've thought a lot about God bein' unfair to black people," Bud says. "I've read about it and I think some place in the Bible has spoken of them days and slavery. Oh it's somethin' about one nation bein' the rulers, and the other nation bein' the hewers of wood and the drawers of water. I think that meant black folks. But I don't know. It do seem like it was unfair."

The Southern Christian church had very little difficulty reconciling itself to slavery and suffering for the black man. It preached a doctrine of reward in the next life for the pain in this one, and that reward would only be gained if the slave behaved himself and obeyed his master. The church's endorsement of the principle of slavery wasn't lost to the black man. There is a very old and cynical slave song:

> White man use whip
> White man use trigger,
> But the Bible and Jesus
> Made a slave of the nigger.

When the burial is over and the oration read, the family lingers, talking quietly; then they embrace and begin to depart to their various near and distant places. When the next one dies, they will gather again. Death marks their reunions and provides the family's continuity. Soon all have gone and Bud and Reverend Alan Lightner remain behind to lock up the church.

Bud and Reverend Lightner discuss some of their church business together. Lightner is a slim, intensely articulate young man. At times, when he talks, you feel that he would like more than one tongue; his words never seem to flow fast enough to capture the ideas he wants to express. He is something of a radical; and has been arrested several times. Once, while the police were handcuffing him, he was jabbed in the thumb with a needle. His arm swelled up and remained swollen for a week. Another time, he was arrested for speeding in his small canary-yellow Datsun. He took away the policeman's gun and ran off with it across the fields. He was finally caught and jailed for a few days. He is one of Arthur's local heroes.

Lightner heads for his car, after shaking hands with us, and hurries off down the road. Bud and I walk slowly around the church, and stare out at the peanut field opposite. The light has begun to fade, and the shadows of the oak mantle the church and the graveyard.

"I remember very clear when Martin Luther King was killed," Bud says. "I was at the market when word came over the radio. I didn't know what to do. I just sat and cried, and then went home without doin' any business. He must have been a God-sent man, that's what I hear everybody say you know. I think he could handle most anythin' the president of the United States could handle I believe, and could probably have done a better job than some of them did. But he didn't last long while he was doin' it, but when he got his job finished, I think the good Lord called him away. He really done a good job while he was doin' it." He stops for a while. "We also had the two Kennedy brothers, and they too was killed for doin' the same thing—tryin' to free the black man."

As the light fades further, the church slowly becomes a part of the shadows and the trees and the darkening sky. It seems to shrink into the evening, and it is difficult to distinguish its outlines.

"I guess why white worship in one church and black in another is 'cause of the different races," Bud says, studying his little church. "That's the way it's been all the time. Sometime they will let a black man in if the board would admit him. We have white people come to our church, lots of times. They just come and we invite them in. But you go to their church you gotta let them know you're comin' and then they have to make arrangements that everybody agrees that you can come in. I couldn't walk into a white church. Not in Eufaula I couldn't. I wouldn't try, not in Eufaula, 'cause I'm not well enough known up there. There's a church right up the road here, Christian Grove, I know pretty well everybody in that church. I might not be too welcome, but I'd go in, if I just wanted to. They may not greet me, and everybody would look strange, y'know, if I walked in. I don't think nobody would attempt to put me out. If I tried that in Eufaula, 'cause I'm not well enough known, they would call a policeman to come and get me."

Reverend Lightner lives about thirty miles from Eufaula. His home is at the end of a dirt road that coils unevenly past deep thickets and woods. When I arrive he is seated at his desk, with a single bare light burning, studying a pile of books. He is married, but I only catch a glimpse of his wife. She hasn't been well, Lightner says, closing his books. They are farming manuals. I had them to be legal tomes for that initial image—young black man, full of rage, the single light—was so intense.

"The white man has taken us out of brutal slavery and

placed us in economic slavery," Lightner says. "I'm a farmer, and the trouble they've given me is incredible. I studied books on farmin', and I applied what I learned, but when they saw I was gettin' to be successful, they started causin' trouble. First, they broke the lease I had, then they wouldn't sell me fertilizer, then they wouldn't buy my crop. They cut my fences and drove their cattle through my peanut fields. Look, I got my documents." He brings them out of a cupboard, pages and pages of leases, farming manuals, fertilizer bills, charges. "I've fought them every inch, and I'll keep fightin' them. I ain't afraid."

The First Presbyterian Church on North Randolph Avenue, in Eufaula, was built in 1869. It is made of brick, imported from Holland, and resembles those small and very pretty churches dotted around the English countryside. In front is a neatly trimmed, extensive lawn that is divided triangularly by two paved paths leading to the entrances of the church. It has a high, square tower, like a battlement, instead of a steeple.

I am here by invitation. Lucien Abraham, a strong church member, wants me to address his Sunday-school class, on Hinduism. I am not sure what I am to tell the children he teaches in a short half an hour on something so alien to this part of the world, but Abraham, quite insistent, says it's going to be a sort of interview.

The interior of the church glitters with polished brass and wood, and the sunlight shining through the Tiffany glass window in front and through the stained-glass windows on the side, falls in mute colors on the carpeted aisle and rows of cushioned pews. The walls soar up to the high, vaulted ceiling, buttressed by arches of exposed walnut wood. "We had Tiffany glass in the other windows, as well," Lucien explains, "but they were damaged by a cyclone back in 1919."

A few members of the congregation are gathered in the

church. They are the Sunday-school pupils. They sing a hymn accompanied by an upright piano. Behind the pulpit is a generously sized organ.

The church has a large number of anterooms and offices. The classes are neatly divided into the various age groups, and each group has its own meeting room. The polished wooden floors of the corridor echo our footsteps. Behind the church, in a neat square, is a well-kept garden. There are benches placed under the shade of the trees, and small pathways wind in between the lawns and the flower beds. The grass is as trim as the lawn in front of the church.

This Sunday-school group is composed of a dozen adults. They are all professional people—salesmen, farmers, small businessmen, secretaries—heartily friendly with each other and this stranger. The classroom is spacious. A long wooden table dominates the room, and enough straight-backed chairs to seat everyone are scattered around the table. Lucien Abraham takes a chair at the head of the table, with me next to him. The others form a semicircle facing him. "One of the reasons we have our guest," Lucien says, "is that, as I explained to him earlier, we as a community seldom get the chance to meet people from other countries, or religions or societies. We are closely knit community, like every other in the South, and we expect everyone else to be the same as us. They are not. I thought this was an opportunity we all shouldn't miss."

Lucien begins by asking questions on religion, but when the floor is thrown open, the discussion drifts from religion to politics and economics and revolution. They are all passionately interested in the plight of the poor in other lands, and why a people rise and overthrow tyrants and emperors. Why communism appeals to the hungry, and not the American way they believe in.

The discussion lasts half an hour, and the moment the allotted time comes, each of the class's members begins to drift to the door one by one. Even on a Sunday there are appointments to be kept, distances to travel.

When I return to the Stanfords, and tell them of my experience and the subjects we talked about, Alma receives the information in silence.

"Did they," Alma finally asks, "talk about the poor in Eufaula, Alabama?"

"No."

CHAPTER 11

Dream House

"C'mon Tavis . . . C'mon Tavis . . . C'mere Tavis . . . C'mon Tavis," Aunt Willie Morris croons and holds out her hands. Tavis turns away, ducks his head into Alma's lap, and refuses to respond. "C'mon Tavis . . . C'mon Tavis . . . C'mon Tavis." The arms remain outstretched, empty.

Arthur's grandaunt on his father's side is in her eighties. We had met earlier at the Stanfords' house, but had had little time to talk. She and Bud were on their way to Doulton to attend a church conference. She is a slim, tall woman with only the slightest stoop. There is beauty not unlike Denise's beneath the creases of age and the wear of hard work. She is an alert active woman who lives by herself about half a mile up the dirt road from the Stanford house. Her house, also raised off the ground a few feet, is wood-framed, and set back from a rough driveway. There is no actual entrance to her yard. The road swerves slightly in token acknowledgment of her house and continues running on. The house is much smaller than the Stanford home. It has a front room with a sofa and a couple of rocking chairs. There is an old blue china washstand and jug standing against a wall, and in a corner, by the window, is a large old record player. It stands chest-high, and is covered by a doily. On one wall are three religious pictures. The bedroom, off to the left, is equally simple. It has a bed and an old black-and-white television. The kitchen is behind the front room.

"I never was lucky," Willie Morris Hamilton says. Her voice quavers slightly with age, the drawl is slower than the others. "C'mon Tavis . . ." He still won't respond. "I've no children. I had eight miscarriages workin' in the fields. Workin' in cotton fields and corn fields and peanut fields. I feel envious of women who have children . . . they have somethin' I never had. C'mon Tavis . . . C'mon Tavis . . . My mother died in 1958 . . . and I was brought up a faithful member of the church. I worked hard all my life . . . choppin' cotton or workin' in peanut fields for my daddy. He never sharecropped. He rented his land from people and we worked on it. He taught me right from wrong. . . . He didn't say much about his daddy or mommy . . . I don't quite remember now after which mommy I was named. Could have been my daddy's. I don't remember much about my granddaddy. They all died when I was young. White folk in those days weren't kind to colored people. No suh! They weren't kind at all. They treated older folk badly, they were rude to them. We had a hard life. We had to take what came. When we took our crop into the market, we never did get what we should've. They always givin' us less. I figured they were cheatin' us for our cotton and our peanuts, but there wasn't nothin' much we could do about that. Yes, I did some schoolin' but not much 'cause I had to help my daddy in the fields. White people are wicked . . . wicked."

Alma and Tavis grow restless. To Alma this story is

130

obviously familiar. She gets up and begins to examine the record player.

"What's this?"

"That's a Victrola," Willie Morris says, and gets up. She goes to Tavis. "C'mon Tavis . . ." But he slides behind Alma. "Here . . . take those things down."

Alma clears the top, opens the cover and peers in. There is a 78-rpm, felt-covered turntable, a speed adjuster, a heavy, round-headed pickup with an old needle stuck in the holder, and a key.

"How does it work?" Alma asks, and frowns at the machine. A faint puff of dust rises from the turntable.

"I think you use the key to wind it up," Aunt Willie Morris says, and picks the heavy metal key up. Except she can't remember where to insert it. We move the Victrola away from the wall and find the hole. I wind it up, and Alma kneels down and opens the cabinet in front. It is filled with old records. Alma is delighted, she has never seen such records before.

"We used to dance to it one time. On Fridays and Saturdays we'd have a few people across and put on them records and dance until late. My husband bought it when we got married. Most people round here had a small Victrola. It was like a small box, not much bigger, and you put it on the table. But my husband wanted this big one so he saved up and bought it in Montgomery. It made a much better sound. Go on . . . play it . . . I haven't heard it for a long time."

Alma and I try to choose a record. Most are unfamiliar and the labels belong to companies which have long since disappeared. The titles are almost unreadable. They've either been scratched by the needle or faded and peeled from age.

"Here," Alma says and picks one at random. She watches with great curiosity as I wind it up, and carefully place the needle on the groove. We all sit back. It's an old blues number. The words, even the music are difficult to make out. There are too many scratches on the record. Alma tries another record. Aunt Willie Morris sits still, her head slightly bent, listening with intense concentration.

"You should get a stereo," Alma says when the record finishes.

"We used to dance to that," Aunt Willie Morris says, not hearing her, but listening to the fading memory of the sounds. "We used to live on Baker Hill then. I've been here . . . eight years. I don't mind livin' alone. I quite like it."

Alma takes Tavis's hand, and moves to the door. Across the road is an empty field that rises gently and then falls away, lost to sight.

"How much land you got Aunt Willie Morris?" Alma asks.

"Oh it's eight acres there and four to that side," she goes out on the porch to survey her land. "My husband bought it. One time that used to be all cotton. I haven't done much with it. Most people round here own their own land, only some rent. So I haven't done nothin' with the land. But I got to keep payin' taxes on it or else they'll take it away from me, and I don't want that to happen. It comes to 'bout sixteen dollars for those twelve acres every year. It's hard findin' that money. I'm gonna leave some of the land to Arthur's [Bud's] children. An acre apiece."

Tavis carefully climbs down the wooden steps and starts running around the yard.

"C'mon Tavis . . . C'mon Tavis . . . C'mon Tavis," she holds out her arms from the porch, but he doesn't want to hear her. Alma also tries to coax him back, but he moves further away. The way children do when they know they're desperately needed.

"Go on Tavis," Alma says, "Go to your grandaunt Willie Morris." Alma forgets that the old woman is Tavis's great-grandaunt. Tavis keeps his distance and there is no way any of us, especially Aunt Willie Morris, can bridge that distance. He will never know her. A good twenty yards and eighty years separates them, and soon it will come to an abrupt end. Possibly when he's older, he'll be told of her by Arthur and Alma, but he will remember little of her. He won't know what it was like to dance to the Victrola. Or to miscarry in a cotton field. Maybe a vague childhood image of an old woman crooning his name and holding out her arms to him, while he dances in the sunlight and kicks up the dust in her yard. He is too young to be interested in the past.

The old woman gives up and retreats to the rocking chair on the porch. Alma catches Tavis, scolds him, but she knows that for some reason of his own, he will not allow his great-grandaunt to hold him, and kiss him, and touch his young face. Aunt Willie Morris accepts the rejection gracefully; it is minor compared to her life. She waves and calls to all of us: "Y'all come back soon now, y'hear."

The little road winds and dips back to the Stanford house. During the rains it must be nearly impassable. There is enough dust to make a good quagmire. Arthur is helping Bud with his car. Odie is working in her back garden with Keith clinging to the hem of her skirt.

Arthur has just returned from Eufaula. He went to inquire about a job with the Alabama Gas Company. It is the only firm in Eufaula that pays wages comparable to the six dollars Arthur made up in Boston. Around six dollars an hour. This wage would enable Arthur to be eligible for the housing loan, or at least decrease his chances for rejection, and to support his wife and child.

"I went into the personnel office," Arthur says, "and The Man asks me if I've already filled in an application form. So I said 'yes. When I was here in May I put in an application for a job with you.' And he says, 'Then you don't want another form. We got no job for you.'" He looks crestfallen and tinkers with the motor a while. Bud remains silent, sympathetic. I feel that if he could, he

133

would move the earth to get his son what he wants. It's so simple, yet unattainable. "I have a friend workin' there," Arthur continues. "He said he'd talk to The Man, but nothin's happened as yet. I don't mind workin' at Roller Die for a while, but it don't pay nothin'. It's got to be temporary till I find somethin' better." He still has a few days before he starts work at Roller Die, but before that he and Alma want to visit Alma's family up in Tennessee. Arthur also wants to return briefly to Boston to wind up all his affairs, pay bills, collect his last salary.

"I'm goin' to keep lookin' even after I start work. I'm workin' nights so I'll spend the day lookin' all around."

"You'll find somethin'," Bud says gently. "You got to have patience."

"Yeah," Arthur says. He must have heard this same advice a dozen times, but he reveals no irritation. He accepts it as gently as his father gave it.

Arthur finishes the job on the car, and we stroll over to the porch. Alma sits in one of the rockers watching the still landscape in front of her. They talk a while about the Alabama Gas Company. The glance she gives is one of disbelief at Arthur's hope of getting this plum job. I wish I had her mastery of expressions, and that toss of her head.

"So what does the white man say?" Arthur asks.

I tell them everything that Lucien Abraham and Ferrel Patrick said. When I finish, Alma snorts.

"I wish you'd taken me to meet them," she says. "I could've had a real fight with them. Progress! Desegregation! Jobs!" She punctuates each with contempt. "If it weren't for the federal government nothing would have happened. We'd still be slaves. You should've let me talk to that . . . Patrick!"

"He wouldn't have said anythin' to you," Arthur says. "Jes' talk round and round. They tell you why I can't get me a loan?, why I can't get me a good job?, why black people don't get nowhere?" Arthur has a long shopping list of resentments, and no one, except those white people in Eufaula, can give him the answers he needs.

Alma sighs. Arthur sits on the swing, pushes gently. I know how they feel; it's as if they've been here an eternity already, and could spend another one doing exactly the same thing.

"You seen where some of the other people live?" Alma asks.

"Those white mansions?"

"Not them. The place by the river. C'mon, we'll show you."

She goes in to change. After a moment Arthur follows her in, taking Tavis with him. It is to be a family outing.

Odie is still working in her garden. It is a fenced-in piece of land just to the rear of the house and towards a stand of trees. She's hoeing in between a row of carrots. Keith has not as yet let go of the hem of her skirt, and she accepts his constant need for attention calmly. She talks to him occasionally, handing him a cookie if he decides to cry.

"I grow my own vegetables most all the summer," Odie says. "And all the winter 'cause I plant turnips in the early fall, so I have vegetables all the year round. I really enjoy my gardenin'. I don't know what I'd do without havin' a garden because I like vegetables and I like to can lots of vegetables. I think I furnish about most of the vegetables for my family out of the garden. My vegetables are much better. They taste better and they're a lot cheaper than they are in the stores. When you go buy them you have to pay so much for the farmer, when I can buy the seeds and grow them much cheaper."

The perspiration begins to run down her face, her glasses slide and she props them back up on her nose. She's cleared most of the dead leaves and weeds down one row and starts down the next without a break. She only stops when Keith begins to cry.

135

"Hush child," Odie says gently. "Go to the house and get some more biscuits. Go . . . get some." He refuses to move, clutching even tighter at her skirt as if the only word he has managed to understand, and knows too well, is the word "go."

"Yes, I believe in God strongly," Odie says. "He will supply you with water when it's needed 'cause He knows better where it's needed than we. I believe the Lord will send the rain in time. I guess I have faith in Him and trust Him and that He will send it in time. We may feel we need it, when He know when we need it better than we know ourselves and so He will send it the time it's needed." She pauses in her work. She straightens, to my eye level, and leans on the hoe. "We think a lot of time we need things when we don't need them and so we'll say 'well we really need the rain,' we say, 'we're gettin' too much of the rain.' So He knows more when we need it and how much we need, and so He sends it just when it's needed. And we trust Him and, of course, there is a lot of people who don't have faith enough to believe that He will do that. But I do."

She returns to her hoeing. She has no doubt of God's existence, nor the nature of His work. In fact, when I think of it in the garden, she has the God of Spinoza, the 17th-century philosopher who believed that God revealed Himself in the structure of nature, and also in the harmony of what exists.

"I feel He is the God of all," Odie continues. "He made us all. He made the white, He made the black, and He mae everybody. And it wasn't intended for us not to get along. That's the weakness of man—the reason we don't all get along. But it's not God's will, 'cause His will is He made us all, and He loves one as much as He loves the other. Man brung about the differences."

"This difference is certainly causing Arthur Dean some problems."

"Well, the white man can make it difficult but in time

they'll get it," Odie says calmly. "But it might not be just when they want it. But they will get the house 'cause they can't hold . . . keep everythin' down from them: can hold them back for a while but they can't keep them back always. They'll get their house . . . I feel like they will. Arthur (Bud) and I will be going to see The Man in the bank, and we're goin' to help Arthur Dean get himself a federal loan. If one turns him down I'm sure someone else will come along and help him."

Arthur wanders over to collect me for the ride. He watches his mother for a minute as she works, and then turns back and heads to his car. Alma and Tavis are already sitting in the car. Odie, in her turn, now watches Arthur. He hasn't told her about the Alabama Gas Company's rejection, but she suspects, possibly in the fractional change in his walk or even something in his face that only she recognizes, that he wasn't successful.

"Eufaula bein' a white town, it's goin' to be kind of difficult," Odie says, not returning to her hoeing, but still watching Arthur, who has poked his head under the car hood once more. "But he won't have to stay in Eufaula all the time to get a job. He can go other places, another town nearby where he can go and get a job. He can go to Abbeville or he can go to Phenix City. He could probably get a job there. There are so many large industrials around where he could get a job. He may have to go further than Eufaula, but he can still build his home here."

"That makes his life more difficult doesn't it?"

"Well, he can get a job, but as you know it won't be one of the best jobs. They'll give him somethin' like Roller Die factory that's not makin' as much money as he wants to make. But he can make out with it, until he can better hisself. He can work on that one and at the same time he can be lookin' for another job, you see, in his spare time. Then if they won't give him the amount of money he wants, he should have, Arthur Dean will just have to get

137

another job somewheres else, and build his home here. He'll still be here." Odie wipes away the perspiration. Her dress clings to her back. "I'll tell you what it needs, it needs more blacks to have businesses of their own. That's what it needs. But they have poor chance among the white. Just a few of the white would be willin' to help us, but they're not goin' to give up too much from each other."

"Is there much dependence, by the blacks on the whites now?"

"Yes, 'cause otherwise it's not goin' to be easy," Odie says. "Unless you got somebody vouchin' for you, it's not easy for no black in Eufaula. They get the jobs but a lot of time they have some white friend that will vouch for them, and get them a good job. There is a few black in Eufaula that can vouch for you as well as a white 'cause they is capable of doin' jobs. Yes, it depends on your connection. Even then, if they got a white goin' for the same job, he'll get the job first, and the black would have to wait."

"Why do you want your son to come back?"

Odie doesn't answer immediately. She begins to hoe again, looking carefully down at the brownish-red earth that is kicked up by the implement. Arthur honks his horn, and Alma impatiently waves for me to join them.

"This is his home," Odie says softly. "He was born here, and his mother, his father, his sisters, all lives here. Everybody's here except one brother, but he's comin' back too. I feel like Arthur Dean would feel more satisfied since he didn't like to be away from home. He'd be . . . most satisfied back home, close to his father and mother, and all his inheritance of what he have. He has a little inheritance here and I think it would be better for him back here."

We drive into Eufaula, and turn east off Route 437. The music from his tape cocoons us off from each other, and I think of how Odie spoke of inheritance not as wealth and possessions but of something more permanent, almost incalculable. The land is history, a family history. It sprawls out from the Stanford home, mostly unused, thicketed, of little cash value. This inheritance is a fabric of land and people. Not just sisters and brothers and aunts but also countless cousins and friends. All of this has somehow got to be kept intact for the next generation, whatever the consequences of a poverty imposed by the white people.

The housing estate that Arthur and Alma want me to see looks still unfinished. A new house is just being completed near the entrance to the curving drive. The white concrete exposed against the red earth looks anemic. Of the single-story houses we pass, some, the more expensive, are on the shoreline of Lake Eufaula. The earth slopes down in immaculate lawns, and when we peer past the patios and the carports and glass-walled living rooms, we can catch glimpses of the water, small jetties, one or two boats, and strips of beach. There is little sign of human activity as we drive slowly down through the estate. It is eerie. A sprinkler throws water out in a sparkling fine spray, a dog lopes after the car, barking.

"Stop," Alma commands. "There it is . . . that's what we're going to have."

She points to a very wide, low house. On either side of the door are huge windows. The front has a small porch, almost, if not quite, resembling a Grecian temple. The four small pillars hold up a triangular roof. The place is deserted and we all climb out. Alma is as excited as any woman who has turned a corner and found permanent enchantment. The curtains on the windows are drawn and though Alma peers in, she can see nothing. Arthur goes round the side, and calls us over. There's a small swimming pool behind a low wooden fence.

"It's exactly what we're going to build," Alma says. "Except they have a carport and I'm going to have a den there. How much you think this one costs?"

"I don' know," Arthur says. "C'mon. Let's go."

Our presence attracts no attention. No heads appear, no human voice can be heard.

"Where's everyone?"

"Watchin' us," Arthur says quietly. "Hopin' we'll go away."

"Let's see what the rest is like," Alma says.

The road curves sharply to the left, and now, with fewer trees, we can see larger patches of water. It looks serene, soothing. At the end of the road, to the left, on the lawn of the very last house is a "For Sale" sign.

"We can find out how much that costs," Alma says, and before either Arthur and I can move she is out of the car and marching up the driveway to the front door. As we hurry after her, we notice the woman opposite. She is in her sixties, white, and clinging to what looks like a fur mat. It stirs and yaps. It is difficult to read the expression on her face from this distance. Except she doesn't move or greet us. She only stands and stares.

The door is opened by a young white woman. She is in her early thirties, and wears shorts and a blouse. Behind her is her husband. He is dressed somewhat similarly: shorts and a shirt.

"I saw your sign," Alma says. "And I wondered whether we could look around."

"Certainly," the husband says from behind, and his wife, after a moment's hesitation, steps aside.

The furniture is too heavy for the house. The chairs, the sofas, the beds, are made of what looks like heavy oak. The colors are dark, brooding, and since the curtains are drawn it feels as if we've stepped into a gloomy cave. It's a family house, with a den, and a dining room and two bedrooms and a vast kitchen. Alma is delighted.

During the tour, neither the husband nor the wife, after their initial hesitation, reveals any hostility towards us. They are from the South, but not Eufaula.

"I'm building a house across on the other side of the

140

lake," he says. "It's gotten a lot more expensive since we began . . . going to cost us seventy thousand now. So we got to sell this one soon."

"How much would this one be?" Alma asks.

"Sixty," he says.

Alma nods as if this figure is well within her means. She is quite enjoying the game, and she takes another quick, critical sweep through the house. As we leave, the woman opposite who's been watching starts to cross over the road, the dog still clutched to her bosom.

We slowly cruise back out of the estate. There is still no sign of life.

"When you look at all this and those white mansions in Eufaula," Alma says, "and all of them owned by white people, it makes you wonder how did they get all this. None of the black people have a fine brick house and whatever. Like on this highway going to Eufaula, like the black people live on the one side of the road and on the other side live the whites. And only a little of the white, the low-class ones, live on the black side. It makes me wonder . . . how did this come about? How did they get everything and the blacks have so little? I think the blacks own more land than the whites, but evidently the whites are using their heads to make money out of their lands and the blacks are not. They're just letting their land sit, and do nothing when the whites are building restaurants and opening movie houses and whatever."

"That's 'cause they won't let us," Arthur says quietly. "You can't get no . . . no . . . money from them to do anythin'."

Momentarily, Alma looses her stride. I can see the faint depression settle, the music does little to alleviate it for a few miles. Even Tavis, trying in his child's way to sing to the music, fails to amuse Alma.

"We don't stand a chance unless the black people stand behind us," Alma finally says. "You and me . . . we can't change Eufaula no way by ourselves, nobody can do

141

nothing by themselves. They can believe in something and do what they have to do, but they can't change unless they have some people to follow them. And like the whites here, they think they're dominant over the blacks, they think they're smarter. I think that a black person, if he really knows what he wants to do and really believes that he can do it, he can do it, no matter how hard a time the white people give him. He can do it."

Her anger is visible and fierce, but brief. Alma knows how to control her bursts of passion and I can see her make a visible effort to calm herself. She succeeds, for after a few moments, she relaxes—hums to the music, talks to Tavis—as if nothing had occurred.

"If you moved into that place back there, you think there'd be any hostility?"

"Oh yeah, but I think a young couple like me and Arthur could cope with it," Alma says, hesitates and continues. "But we would cope with it up to a point, and then we would probably move or sell or whatever, but we would like to give it a try. I think we would stay there longer than an older couple, because they would feel why should they have to take it and they'd leave without giving it a chance."

"I thought that couple were pretty nice," Arthur says. "I mean . . . they didn't refuse or nothin'."

"They were nice," Alma agrees. "I think we could move there. I don't think they'd appreciate it if we was a huge family with a lot of kids, older kids, and stuff running around. But I think we could make it there, probably would be hard but we could make it. I wouldn't quit easy. I feel the blacks here somehow they are afraid to really open up and to let the whites know where they're coming from. They let the white people get away with a lot of things they shouldn't. They should open their mouths and speak up, and maybe things would change then. But until they do, things are going to be the

142

same in Eufaula. We got to let them know where we're coming from."

"Not that we can afford it," Arthur Dean says, "but if we could I'd sure move in there. They probably wouldn't want us there, but that wouldn't affect me." He pauses, mulling it over. "But I prefer more or less the country itself."

On the way back home, we stop off at a small restaurant on Route 437. It's an old, homely looking building, set a few yards back from the road. It is also quite empty, and after we've taken a table, an old straight-backed white woman hurries in from the rear. She reminds me of a seedy English aristocrat. She has a smile, but it fades when she sees us. Arthur Dean and Alma grin at her discomfort. She serves in silence, takes the money in silence, watches us leave in silence. I am getting used to the treatment, and we spend the rest of the journey home chuckling over her reactions. Arthur Dean does a takeoff that makes Alma laugh. Tavis, presumably also thinking it good, falls off the seat laughing.

The school bus is gone when we return. Bud, punctual and dependable, has gone to drive the kids back to their homes from school. Arthur Dean decides to show me where he's going to build his home, if he can ever get his loan. It's nearer the road than the old house, and would sit squarely on the weed patch.

"I'm kind of hopin' the house will sit right beyond the sticks and go back into the woods, to the edge. It'll start from over there, where the pecan tree stands, and reach out right along here." He paces the earth, marking out the boundary of the house. The weeds reach his waist. "I'm goin' to have to clear off some of these trees, so I can get quite a bit of yard space. And over here I want to have a large flower garden, so it'll be pretty, y'know."

He looks back towards the old house, beyond the

shadows of the pecan trees. His home would be sixty yards away, and each morning when he woke he would be able to look across and see his father and mother begin their day.

"And it'll be satisfyin' livin' on the land, amongst my family."

CHAPTER 12

Memphis, Tenn.

Since we arrived in Eufaula, Alma has been fretting to visit her family. Arthur, with a few days remaining before he joins Roller Die, needs to return to Boston to pick up his salary and settle a few bills, and to end their life there. He decides to go via Memphis.

We should have begun the trip to Memphis after breakfast, but in the manner of all those well-planned journeys, there were minor delays such as waking late, having the car cleaned, an errand or two to be run. It is three hours past noon when Arthur Dean slides behind the wheel. It is an eight-hour drive from Eufaula, Alabama to Memphis, Tennessee, and this means most of the journey will take place in the dark.

"That don't make me too happy," Arthur says. "I don't like drivin' through Mississippi at night. They don't like us much, and the whites can cause trouble if somethin' should happen." Route 431 takes us back into Eufaula where we pick up Route 82 for Montgomery. From there we're to take Route 65 to Birmingham, and then Route 78 to Memphis. Route 78 passes through Tupelo. "That's one town I drive real careful in. 'Specially with the problems there now." He is referring to the trial of a black youth on a rape charge.

"Go through at ninety," Alma suggests from the back seat.

Arthur and Alma are well prepared for the journey. They have a foot-high stack of tapes for themselves and for Tavis a box full of toys. He is a seasoned car traveler. This confined space causes him no problems. If it's not his toys or the music, he waves to passing cars. I watch the landscape during these daylight hours. It is unvaryingly beautiful and rich, and it isn't hard to imagine this land, not long ago, to have been uninhabited. No scars of civilization, no highways, no pylons. It is impossible to imagine Europe or Asia as ever having been empty, the past has too tight a grip on the imagination. There is so little open space and every acre of land has been used and reused for centuries. There is too much space here for the dust of the past to have accumulated and blurred the imagination. It still remains a place of emptiness.

But a more distant past has been idling in Arthur Dean's imagination.

"You ever been to Africa?" Arthur asks.

"Parts of it."

"You know, I sometimes wonder what . . ." he hesitates, concentrates on his driving for a while, ". . . I would be if I'd been born there. You know, my ancestors not . . . havin' been brought across as slaves."

"What do you figure?"

"I could have been an . . . anything, right? I could've been a chief or a general or a . . . hunter. Yeah. I could've been a hunter like I see in those pictures."

"Hunter? What do you want to think about all that for?" Alma asks indignantly.

"I could have been, couldn't I?" Arthur asks wistfully, ignoring Alma's practicality.

"You could have. You could have been a diplomat or a Nyerere or a guerrilla soldier. You would have belonged to one tribe or another, to one country, to one land, where everyone was the same as you. You might not have become anyone famous or notorious, but you would have a sense of permanence for the people and the land. When you are in exile—and that is what you are in . . . Malcolm X wrote: 'No matter how long you and I have been here, we aren't Americans'—you can never find a permanent warmth."

"Yeah, I know," Arthur nods. "If I was livin' in Africa I would come to this country to study. I've seen African students in Boston; they get treated different from us. They get a lot of respect, y'know. Yeah, I wouldn't mind comin' here as one of them students. It wouldn't be too bad then, livin' in this country, 'cause when I finish I could go home. I wouldn't stay at all, I'd go back to my country . . . an' do somethin' for it."

"Oh you keep dreaming," Alma says. "You can't go back to Africa."

"I didn't say I was goin' back to Africa," Arthur Dean says patiently. "I said if I was African, I'd come here and then go back. You're not listenin'. Right?"

"Right."

"What's the good of thinking of all that?" Alma says. "You're not African; you're a nigger here. There is no Africa for us. And we can never go back. Least, I wouldn't."

"Even to visit?"

"I wouldn't mind," Arthur says.

Alma shrugs, not having given it that much thought. "No. Maybe. But it wouldn't be like here, would it. That would be like what you said. Being in exile, but over there."

"I'd just like to see what it's like," Arthur says. "To see where my people come from. Most probably I got cousins and relations there . . . not that I'd recognize them or they me. We'd be distant, y'know."

"Distant!" Alma echoes mockingly and turns away. She sighs suddenly, and slumps in the seat. "God it's so hard being a minority. You gotta keep fighting all the time. You got to do better than white folk, you got to be sharper than them. Isn't that true?"

"Yes. You have to excel, while they can merely be good at something. You cannot be their equal, whether in athletics or in intelligence. You have to be superior, before they'll give you a break."

The shadows are deepening, darkening. The sun, no longer gold, is sinking down behind the trees like a tired, bloodshot eye; perfect in roundness, the edges so clear and distinguishable. Tavis sleeps, and Alma fiddles with the dial of the radio. The highway begins to sparkle with the lights of motorcars, and soon that dusk has turned to darkness. Arthur Dean is driving fast and well, and often he reaches out for his CB radio to talk to cars coming south to check that there is no sign of Smokey. There is a certain democracy in these short, disembodied conversations; black and white cut in with information. They sound like prey in a forest full of shadows and dangers calling to each other that a predator is out and prowling. Only those who have no ear for this crackling jargon will be caught in those waiting traps.

Our conversation drifts to the Queen of England. Arthur is under the impression that everyone in that country has to send her a certain amount of money, or else part of their farm crop. Alma pulls his leg about seeing too many Robin Hood films. The conversation drifts further onto the occult, reincarnation, religion. We cross the state line into Mississippi, and immediately Arthur drops his speed down to fifty-five miles an hour. Here he doesn't even trust his unseen informants on the

CB. It could be imagination, but they both become quieter, and Arthur even more watchful.

"I don't like drivin' through here at night at all." Arthur says quietly. He sounds like a boy passing through a graveyard.

I catch his mood; quiet, watchful, though I'm not sure what I'm looking for. There is little that can be seen outside the straight shafts of light ahead; to the sides are only varying degrees of blackness.

Arthur suddenly breaks the silence: "I got to fill the tank."

"Do we have to?" Alma asks. "Can't you wait until we get into Tennessee?"

"No. Better do it here than stop in Tupelo."

Out of the darkness, we see a shallow pool of light. There are two gas pumps under it, and beyond is a small diner. We can see half a dozen white men, some in overalls, sitting on the stools, and hear the faint strains of the jukebox. The car crunches on the gravel and quietly stops at the pumps. All this light is encircled by the night. As Arthur is about to climb out, there is a sudden burst of violence in the diner. It happens too quickly to register. A body stumbles through the door, slides and slips and finally sprawls on the gravel. It is followed by a tall, thickset man wearing a short-sleeved shirt. He stoops, picks up the body, sets it on its feet, and shoves it towards the parked pickups hidden deeper in the shadows.

"Get out and stay out."

"Ah'm sorry . . . ah'm sorry." The body becomes a youth in his early twenties. At first I think he's too drunk to even stagger, but as he moves to his pickup, mumbling his apologies, I notice his limp. One leg is much shorter than the other.

"Oh God." Alma whispers, and slides down in her seat. "Let's get out of here."

Arthur hesitates, then shakes his head, and continues

149

out. He looks tense, half-afraid, but determined. He ducks his head back in.

"Find out where the washroom is," he tells me.

The bouncer has returned to the diner. A few of the men who'd stood up to watch the scene have settled back on their stools. I approach it uneasily. I've seen too often how contagious violence can be; and how exciting for the participants. Alma's fear has also touched me. But what makes me hesitate the most is the reputation of the South. It is a dark, violent one, full of casual killings; sudden and unrepentant. There is a madness loose here and even the stranger has no immunity from it. My approach is noticed, first by the bouncer behind the counter, and then by those on the stools. It is a silent signal, for I can see nothing spoken; only the heads, one by one, turning to watch me. I open the door. The room is small, and narrow and warm. It smells of cigar smoke. There is a silence, in spite of the jukebox mindlessly vomiting its music.

"Where's the washroom?" I hear my exaggerated English accent.

The heads, as one, cock to my voice, puzzling out its origins, and then all turn to the man behind the counter, as if for translation.

He points. "Round the corner."

I step gratefully back into the night, and pass the information on to Arthur who wakes Tavis and takes him to the washroom. Alma refuses to get out of the car at all.

We pass through Tupelo with no incidents. Arthur drives extremely cautiously, and the town, small and indistinguishable in the night, is soon behind us. We reach Memphis around midnight.

Smithridge Road, in north Memphis, is a clean tree-lined street. On either side are small, one-story brick houses with shingles on the roofs, and small front yards. The area is mainly black populated, and blue-collar, and very urban. It is such a contrast to the Stanford landscape in Alabama. Alma's parents live in a neat white house. It has a tree in the front yard and children playing on the grass. The house looks as if it could be a trailer home; it has the shape and those same spare, straight lines, lacking only the wheels. Even the door is made up of that same fragile metal.

The front room is small. There is a large comfortable sofa against the wall opposite the front door, and to one side, a smaller one and a black leather easy chair—the kind that when you lean back a footrest materializes from underneath. A dining table is set against the window looking out on the yard and beyond, and part of the room is the kitchen. Between the two is a door that leads back to the bedrooms. The presence of children is very evident; a few toys lie around, a coloring book, half-crayoned, is open on the coffee table.

Ruby Glover, Alma's mother, is a large, friendly woman. She's taller than Alma, and certainly doesn't look her age or reflect the exhaustion of having borne ten children. She does have the same hidden sensuality that I've noticed in Alma, a sort of langour which is never shaken by playing children or neighbors dropping in and out.

"I've been workin' all my life," Ruby says. The Tennessee accent, a drawl, is harsher than the Alabaman. It sounds more nasal, as if this far from Alabama, the accent has been changed by its proximity to the northern states. "We were very poor, and we lived in Tipton County. That's about thirty miles north of here. I had to walk to school, rain or shine, and in the winters I remember we'd get to school and my feet felt as if they'd been cut off at the ankles. We only had two pairs of shoes a year, and we'd have to take them off and dry them while we sat in class. They never did get dry in time, so when we started back, they'd be cold and wet. Often, we didn't have much food in the house. There used to be a dewberry tree outside our home and often I'd see my mother go out and pick the best dewberries that tree had and put them in a pan of water and cook them. We'd have a dewberry stew and eat some bread with it. Sometimes, we had nothin'. But I'm not sayin' I was unhappy as a child. We used to have good fun . . . we was never bored as the kids are today. All they want to do is watch television. We used to make swings out of the vines and play a lot.

"On my mother's side, my grandfather and grandmother died before I was born, so I don't know much about them. I did know my grandfather and grandmother on my father's side, but they didn't tell us much, 'cept it was hard. Real hard. The white man was never kind to black folk, they made life more difficult than it needed to be. Well, even my mother never told me much about her life . . . what it was like when she growed up. I've asked her . . . and all she will say is 'It was fine.' Nothin' more than that, and I know it wasn't fine. How could it be? We used to have to buy our clothes from the orphanage for fifty cents, because we had no money for better things and when I was ten, maybe eleven years old, I'd work six to six choppin' cotton and makin' one dollar for a day's work. And this was apart from walkin' all the way to the fields . . . Sometimes it was four to five miles away so we had to wake long before six to get there in time. And if you didn't pick the cotton, the white man would make you leave the house and give it to another, so we had to keep workin' in order to live in the house. I'm fifty-three now and I'm doin' household work in the town for my livin'."

This is Alma's home. She didn't grow up here, but she is visibly at ease, while Arthur is formal, and quiet. Tavis plays with her younger brother and sister, Bobby and Janice. They are ninth and tenth in the seniority ladder, and one is eight, the other eleven. Ruby has prepared a huge dinner. Lawrence and Annie, Alma's older brother and sister, need to be picked up.

Anne is a pretty, square-faced girl with very close-cut hair. She is as heavily built as her mother, and is delighted to see Alma again. They haven't seen each other for months, and chatter away in the back seat of Arthur's car as we drive around looking for Lawrence. Annie is going through a particularly difficult period in her life. She has been looking for a job for months and not had any luck.

"I'm sure not goin' back to pickin' cotton or pickin' anythin'," Annie says. "But it's got to the point I'm figurin' on signin' up with the Army. Least you get some money and maybe I'll even do some travelin'."

"You don't want to join the Army?" Alma says in horror.

"Why not? There's nothin' else around here in Memphis," Annie says. "I swear I've been out lookin' every day . . . anythin' at all I'll take, but there's nothin' for a nigger girl. No one will give me a job. I'm goin' to go down into Mississippi tomorrow 'cause I heard they were hirin' in a factory. I don't like to work in Mississippi, but it's better than havin' nothin'."

"You should come down with us to Eufaula, and get a job in Roller Die," Alma suggests.

"I sure don't want to go down to no Alabama," Annie says. "Things are worse down there for us black folk than it is in Tennessee."

"It's not that bad," Arthur protests.

Lawrence is the spitting image of the Bear. He is as broad as he is tall, and the springs of the car compress a couple of inches when he climbs in. Lawrence has had a very late night. In fact, although it is now past four, his night has just come to an end. He's been playing poker and appears to have had some luck in the cards. He gives Alma a friendly pat in greeting, and she pulls his leg all the way back to the house about his high living.

"You a drinkin' man?" Lawrence asks me.

"Yes."

"Stop off, Arthur," Lawrence, "I think he needs to taste some pure Tennessee whiskey."

Lawrence ducks into a liquor store and returns clutching a bottle. It is only the late afternoon, and I'm not sure I'm up to any experiments with Tennessee whiskey.

"Stop spoiling him," Alma says, and refuses to allow him to pass over the bottle.

It is at dinner that I finally get to meet Alma's father, Steve. He has spent most of his life working in Chicago, and Alma only recalls his occasional visits home during his vacations. There is a certain withdrawn distance to the man. He is plump, with a moustache; round-faced, with deep introverted lines around his mouth, and very quiet. He wears a Panama hat, quite battered and worn, even in the house, and smokes or sucks at a pipe. The family seems to work around him without ever including him in. His time away from them has extracted its price; he could just as well be a stranger. He's been on social security since an industrial injury, and spends most of his days with a brother. They both drive up daily to Tipton to visit with the rest of his family. He takes off his hat to eat dinner, quietly and quickly, and then, after smoking a plug of tobacco, he leaves without a word.

Tipton County, named after Jacob Tipton, a man who raised a company for the defense of the Northwest Territories against the Indians and died leading an attack in 1879, is thirty miles north of Memphis. The county was a big cotton-producing area and its need for slaves was insatiable. In 1840 there were 3,637 whites, 3,132 slaves and 31 free blacks living in the county. In 1860, there were 5,408 whites, 5,288 slaves owned by 469 of the whites, and 9 free blacks. In 1939, there were 11,275 black people and they constituted well over 41 percent of the county's population.

Anne, having little to do except continually search for a job, has decided to join us on our trip to Tipton County. Tavis is left behind with his grandmother. The journey is, for both women, a return to their childhood. They were born in Tipton, and grew up within the family settlement. At Atoka, a couple of miles off Highway 51, is the church where Alma and Arthur were married.

"Let's see if it's open," Alma says, and pushes on the door.

The church looks new, and well looked after. It is made of brick and gleams comfortably in the afternoon sun. There is no formal entrance to its grounds, just a gravel drive and beyond, at the sides and behind, marking its boundaries, a wire fence. Most of the land surrounding the church has been cultivated, except a clump of trees a hundred yards behind. They sit in a small vale.

Alma tries the front door. It is locked. So are the side doors. She is disappointed. It was the scene of their marriage, though not of her baptism or youth. An older, wooden church once stood on this site and on the stone tablet inlaid in the brick by the door are the names of her family who donated money for this new building. Aunts, uncles, cousins, distant friends. Alma recognizes all of them. To the right of the church, at a discreet distance, is the family graveyard. A few have marble headstones, some stone, some a board of wood. The Lemmons have been buried here for over a century.

A quarter-mile up the macadam road, Alma makes Arthur pull off and turn into a cotton field.

"Remember this, Annie," Alma says as we climb out.

"That's where we were born and lived," Annie says, pointing to a stand of trees matted with foliage. It is well behind a cotton field, and as we move towards the trees, through the cotton, with a spaniel pup which has appeared from nowhere to first snap at our heels and then to just idly follow, the two girls strike out at the bushy plants. They seem to be getting back at the plant that once held such power over their lives and the lives of their parents and grandparents.

"There wasn't all this cotton when we was young," Alma says. "It was mostly empty field, so we could play out here."

She doesn't elaborate, she is never to give me details of this childhood apart from her one remark that her family was "dirt-poor."

"We didn't get to play all that much," Anne says, "'cause we all had to do some work as well. We'd have to work around the house, fetch water, clean, run errands, and then when we was old enough, we had to work in the fields."

The lives of the poor are spare. They live, tightly bound, within the framework of work and exhaustion. Six to six leaves so little time to dream, to dance, to study, to journey to distant places. There is too little time remaining before the welcome of sleep to recall all the dry details of the passing days.

It is only when we have nearly passed through the whole cotton field and neared the clump of trees, that I begin to see the outlines of what was once Alma's home. It is the ruins of a two-story, wood-framed house. The timber has rotted, the floor sags like a hammock. If there was glass in the windows, there is no trace of it now. The roof is made up of sheets of tin, and I would imagine in the summers this place must have been a furnace. The side of the house faces us, the door is hidden by the undergrowth and it is impossible to enter. Not that Alma even wants to. She remains at a safe distance, as if to come nearer is to be reclaimed by this wreck. If there are any pleasant memories of this place, they are not to be read in her face.

"God, it's changed," Annie says. "There wasn't all this stuff around . . . and behind there, you can't see from here, is the well we had to fetch water from every day. It used to be lived in first by the white boss man, then when he moved out, they gave it to us."

"You never showed me this place before," Arthur says quietly. He stands beside her, hands in his pocket, solemnly studying the framework of the house.

"What for?" Alma arches her neck and glances at him. "You expect to find a plaque here, saying Alma lived here." She turns away. "Let's get away from here."

It only takes a dozen yards, and the house fades into the trees and vines. Soon it will be part of them, pulled down and reclaimed by the undergrowth. It is only Pharaohs and white folk who can afford to leave monuments to mark their existence on earth.

The road now winds through gentle country. The fields are small and neat, almost European in their dimensions. There isn't the same expanse of space and the unruliness of nature as around Arthur's home. We pass a diner and a grocery store, and then the road turns sharply left and the tar dissolves into dirt. The dust is thick and red. It is churned up by a dragline scooping gravel and filling a huge mack truck. Other trucks wait in line. The land around here is ugly; most has already been consumed by the bite of the great bucket, and the earth looks raw. The destruction runs for a mile or so past shallow, rain-filled ponds and then, just as I begin to think it will never stop, we pass a curve and come on a small, neat settlement.

The half a dozen houses sit on their own small individual plots of land. Each has a small yard, a garden of flowers, a pathway to the door. The houses are all similar. They too look like trailer homes. Sharp, straight lines, few frills, mesh doors, gently sloping shingle roofs. Each couldn't have more than four rooms. Behind, the land rises somewhat sharply, and at the top of the rise, just in front of a stand of trees, is one other house. It looks down on the others as if separate yet still a part of the gathering below. In the center of the grounds, so each has access, is a vegetable garden. It looks well watered and well tended. There are no shops or stores. I feel as if this little community of houses has hacked its way to a distant frontier, circled in on itself very much like those wagon trains under attack, and have no wish to socialize with the rest of the world.

All the inhabitants of the houses are Lemmons. Here are Alma's grandmother and grandfather, aunts, uncles, grandaunts and granduncles. Her father's family, the Glovers, also come from Tipton county, but live much nearer to the church we'd visited.

The sound of the car on the dirt road attracts the attention of one of the inhabitants. The door of the first house, the one nearest the road and riding point, opens, and a tall black man appears and slowly makes his way down the steps. He is Ike Lemmon, Alma's grandfather. He is very spare and very dark. He has a small, neat face, quite square, and well lined. His teeth have rotted, and when he smiles in recognition of Alma, I can see large gaps. He wears a sweat-stained baseball cap and his jacket hangs loose on his frame. His rubber boots reach halfway up to his knees. He hugs both his granddaughters, and shakes Arthur's and my hand. The palms of his hand are hard and calloused.

"You been out, Grandpa?" Alma asks.

"Been pickin' cotton," Ike Lemmon says, and laughs. "Way up there." He points back up the road. He talks softly and punctuates his sentences with short laughs; it is difficult to understand all of what he says, as he fades quite suddenly as if forgetting what he is talking about.

"How much they paying?" Alma asks.

"Three dollars," Ike says. "I been up there at five this mornin', and I just got back."

"You don't have to work," Anne says indignantly.

"No, I don't, but I got myself tired sittin' round the house so I do some work when I can."

"How old are you?" Alma asks.

158

"Well into my eighties," Ike says, "but I can't remember 'xactly." He stops, considering the horizon. "Maybe eighty-one or eighty-two. I guess workin' just gets to be a habit." He laughs again, this time it is out of the pure pleasure of having visitors.

We follow him up the three steps to his house, and into the front room. It is very simply furnished with an old sofa and opposite it, a couple of chairs and coffee table. Towards the back of the room is the dining table. And on the walls are framed religious pictures.

"Yassuh, I'll keep pickin' cotton until the day I die," he sits down in one of the straight-backed chairs formally as if he is the visitor to this house, not us. "And then I work on our land some. We got sixty-two acres, and grow most of our own vegetables."

"Where's Grandma?" Annie asks.

"Inside," pointing to another room.

As if she'd been waiting in the wings, Willie May Lemmon comes in from the kitchen carrying a hamper of wet laundry. She is a small woman, about half the height of Ike. Her head is covered with a scarf, and her face, small with high cheekbones, is closed. Her mouth is a firm, straight line. She is alert in a snappy way, and brusque, though affectionate, in her embrace of Annie and Alma and Arthur. Her hand feels, if not as calloused, at least as worn and used as her husband's. She sits, but it is with the air of a woman interrupted mid-chores who wishes she'd been informed of the visit well in advance.

"What are you doin' here?" she asks Alma. "How's Boston?"

"Didn't you know? We've moved to Eufaula."

"That's good. I never like you all far away. Now you can visit more often, can't you?" she turns to Arthur.

"Yes ma'am," Arthur says dutifully.

"Got a job as yet, Annie?"

"No, Grandma. I been lookin' and lookin', but no one wants me," Annie says.

159

Ike sits quietly, effectively out of the small gossip of the three women, and I ask him softly how long he's been married now.

"Oh, let's see . . . a long time," he brightens and leans forward to talk. "Got married way back in the '20s when . . ."

"Oh shut up, Ike," Willie May Lemmon says briskly, and obediently he sits back and falls into a shy silence.

The two girls look faintly embarrassed, but certainly not surprised by their grandmother's action. I feel I've broken some secret family rule, and try to engage Willie May in conversation. She is wary and if not quite monosyllabic in her replies, certainly uninformative.

"I've had a happy life," she keeps repeating as if it has been drilled into her. "It's been a good life for me. I got no complaints."

I feel like an interrogator asking a prisoner of war for enemy positions, only to receive a name, rank and serial number. Alma and Annie try to come to my aid, but they also receive the same treatment. When I look around for Ike, he's gone. Grandma's impatience with the visit becomes more and more visible. She keeps glancing towards her laundry and round the room, and soon, unable to sit any longer, she moves to the hamper and picks it up. It is our signal of dismissal, and on the way up the hill to the small house at the top, Alma and Anne keep apologizing.

"She's always like that to Granddad," Annie says. "Whenever he opens his mouth, she tells him to shut up."

"That's why he keeps workin'," Arthur says.

"Yeah. It keeps him out of the house, and away from her," Alma says. "And she never talks about her life to us. Granddad does . . . when he gets the chance, but she never says anything. I mean she's afraid, y'know what I mean. In case the white people hear she talked, and

160

they'll fire her. She's workin'in a house . . . cleaning and stuff." She says this with disgust.

"What's she got to be scared about?"

"The old folk are always scared of the white man," Annie says. "You got to behave . . . you got to behave . . ." She mimics her elders. "What for? You get nothin' out of them anyway. The old folk been scared so long, they think we got to be scared as well." She sighs and kicks at a stone. I would suspect that she is normally a cheerful girl, but the specter of her constant unemployment turns her gloomy often. Her chances of getting a job will always remain slim; black unemployment in America runs to thirty-eight percent. Depressing, Depression figures.

There are children playing outside the house on top of the hill, and the moment they see Alma and Annie they run in to tell their mother. It's only as I get nearer, I notice that this is a trailer home. The wheels have been removed and the base now sits on blocks.

In contrast to Ike and Willie May's home, this house is filled with furniture. There are sofas, easy chairs, tables, statuettes of religious figures standing wherever they can stand, pictures of Jesus and Mary on the walls, and a generously proportioned television set. The impression of overcrowdedness could be because of the smallness of the room, and the number of children who've decided to stop playing to join Alma and Annie inside.

Aunt Bernice is Alma and Annie's favorite aunt. She is a slim woman with a pretty, oval face. She resembles Alma more than any other member of the family I've met so far. And she appears to have been granted perennial youth. Alma guesses her to be in her fifties, but here appearances are most deceptive. I would have guessed her to be around thirty, especially as there are a couple of children in their very early teens. But there is an elder son, in his thirties, visiting from Chicago. She is a

161

bustling, energetic woman, and full of opinions.

"Oh that woman," she says when Alma tells her about Grandma Willie May. "Happy life? She doesn't know what she's talkin' about. I should know, I'm her daughter. I've seen her work from dawn to night, at home, in the fields, back at home . . . not one day of rest, and never enough food to put on the table at the end of the day. She's led a hard, hard life, but she can't admit it to herself, or to us. I don't know anythin' about her life before I was born or what her mother told her about her own life. She never talks about that. She's ashamed of it, she's ashamed of bein' poor, she's ashamed that life should've been so cruelly hard. So when anyone of us ever asks her, what her life has been like, she'll say it was a good life. I don't think she even wants to think about it. She works three days of the week in a white family's house, they don't pay her much, and she has to cook and clean. I've been there, and she's always tryin' so hard to please them . . . and she says 'yasma'm, yassuh' . . . it breaks my heart to see that. She don't want anyone to talk about her life . . . that's when dad tries to say anythin' she tells him to shut up. He never gets to say much in the house, not in all the time I was growin' up."

I am reminded of a line from Faulkner's *The Sound and the Fury:* "They were black: They endured." I had not understood her reticence before and now, though I have been given only the briefest sketch of her life by her daughter, I can see why this past will always remain hidden. Endure! When I first read that line I thought of rocks, and trees and the earth. And pain. It conjures up an outside stillness, an interior of tears.

Alma and Annie find an album of photographs tucked away in one of the shelves, and start turning over the stiff pages. They are both delighted by their discovery, and keep showing me and Arthur Dean distant relatives and friends whom they haven't seen for years.

"When I was eleven," Bernice says, "and I was workin'

in the cotton fields a white man from the North asked me if he could take my photograph." She sighs. "I suppose he must have published it in some magazine showin' this little colored girl at work. I always wonder whether I'll ever get to see that picture one day. That man who took the picture was the only white man I know who showed some courtesy. White people round here just were not good to black people. You had to do what they told you, or else you got into trouble. I worked in those fields, and couldn't finish school 'cause of them. They went to school, they had everythin'. We had nothin'. When I was sixteen, George began courtin' me, and that was a real adventure for me. It was excitin'. We courted for a couple of years, then we was married. It didn't make much difference. I still had to keep workin' in the fields. Even after I had my first baby, I was back in the fields. I used to leave him under a tree and all the folk would keep an eye on him. Then when I had my second child . . . my first was old enough to keep an eye on him. I remember once, when I was workin' at the far end of the field, someone came runnin' to tell me my baby had gone. I ran back, and found that my older boy had buried the baby in the sand. Nothin' happened to the baby, thank God, but boy did I whup George."

George laughs. He is a heavily built man with strong arms and shoulders. The easy chair can just hold his frame.

"Didn't I?" she asks him.

"I don't remember," he says, "but if you say you did, you did."

Bernice looks pleased at this compliance. "See, everyone knows that I'm a straight-talkin' woman," she says. "I don't take nonsense from anyone, even the whites. I remember years ago standin' in a line in a store, and this white man pushed me out of it. He thought he should go before. I was pregnant at the time, but I pushed right back, and was he surprised. I thought he was goin' to strike me, but he changed his mind. Oh things have changed since those days when the white man just about owned black people. I'm not talkin' slavery times. I'm talkin' twenty, thirty years ago. Things have got better. We're still not equal in economic opportunity to the white man. Maybe it'll come one day. I'm workin' lookin' after this white woman. She's old, and she's rich, and sometimes she tries to get uppity with me, callin' me a nigger or somethin'. I don't care. She needs me more than I need her. She's got no one, I got a whole family, and I told her one day 'now you just stop all that or I'll quit, and you'll not find anyone else,' and she at once changed and began cryin' and asked me not to leave. These white people," she shakes her head in puzzlement.

"They're all like that," George says. "You can't trust them."

He is visiting from Chicago, and comes fairly regularly to see his parents. He would, he says, far prefer to live back South, rather than in the ghetto he inhabits in Chicago.

"That's why we moved back South," Arthur says, looking up from the photo album. There are some pictures of their wedding in it. He is pleased that someone else agrees with his decision. "We're now in Alabama."

"I'm not sure I like Alabama," Bernice says. "Life's tougher down there for blacks. Worse in Mississippi, of course."

"It ain't bad," Arthur says defensively. "An' my family got land there too."

Alma remains neutral in the discussion. She finishes with the album, and she and Annie decide they want to visit Aunt Ella Sadlers. She calls her an aunt, though from another short discussion it turns out to be a great-grandaunt who lives with her nephew, Bill Lemmon. Bill is Ike's brother.

"If you want to talk to my father," Bernice says, "you'll

have to have him up here. And my mother mustn't know about it. He goes off to work very early in the mornin' and I never know which field he'll be workin' in, but I'll arrange it."

It is to take a few days to maneuver Ike Lemmon out from the hold of his wife, and sneak him up the hill.

Great-grandaunt Ella's place is half a mile up the road. The road is all dirt and gravel, and Arthur doesn't want to drive down it. The three of us walk down the road and then cut through a plucked cotton field and waist-high weeds. The dust around us is fine as pollen, and the hum of the insects soothing. The house sits on a slope, shaded by trees and looks deserted. A dog comes out in a rush, and then only sniffs at our heels before wandering away to examine more interesting things.

"If you get a job down in Alabama," Annie says, "let me know, so I'll come down and get one too."

"Sure," Alma says. "You got to come and visit anyway, and you can stay when we build our own house. That won't take too long."

This house is built of timber, with a tar paper roof. It is low and long. A porch runs in front and down one side of the house. A couple of rockers sit out on the porch. The house needs a fresh coat of paint for the board has worn smooth and has mellowed to almost black.

"It's the oldest house around here, isn't it?" Alma asks Anne.

"It's about eighty years old," Annie says.

"Is that all," Alma sounds disappointed. "I was sure it was much older. A hundred maybe."

The interior is cool, and sparsely furnished. In the sudden change of light I can only see a few bits of old furniture, and no one else. Alma calls a couple of times, and it's only when we fall silent we can hear the sound of a television, coming from the next room.

The only light in the room is the chilly gray from the black-and-white television set. A very old woman sits not more than two feet from it. Behind her is a neatly made single bed, and to one side a couple of chairs and a table. The rest of the space is cluttered with cartons and a cupboard and an old wood-burning stove. A few feet away from the woman, though not quite in line with the television set, is an equally old man. Aunt and nephew look as if they have inhabited the earth forever. The sound from the television set is regularly interrupted by the "brr-brr" of scratching. It is a monotonous sound, smooth at times, then stopping and when it starts its pitch is near frantic. Bill Lemmon suffers from a skin rash. There is no cure for it, nor is there any relief.

"Don't get to sleep much 'cause of this," he says very softly, preoccupied with rubbing a plastic scouring pad over his arms and legs, and then inside his shirt. He is small, wasted, almost hidden in clothes a couple of sizes too large for him. They must have fitted him once. All his energy is spent soothing the itch. "Tried everything the doctor gave. Oil, ointments, powder. Nothin' helps . . . I can't concentrate 'cause of it." For a moment, there is silence, then he starts again, not methodically, but randomly, unsure from which direction the next itching attack will come.

Arthur is sympathetic, and when the old man gets up to fetch some water, he hurries ahead of him to help. Alma and Annie sit near their grandaunt. She is watching a wrestling show, and is alert enough to keep a stream of lewd remarks about the physiques of the young wrestlers appearing on the screen. Her comments, whispered, keep the two girls giggling throughout the visit. Unfortunately, Aunt Ella cannot concentrate for long on any subject, and soon she has fallen asleep to the sound of the commentator announcing the winner's name, and the monotonous "brrr-brr-brr" of plastic on skin.

There are other aunts and uncles and cousins and second cousins to visit in the small community and Alma and Annie are embraced and kissed by all. Arthur is, at times, only vaguely recognized, and he, in turn, cannot distinguish one uncle from another or one cousin from the next. They are a sea of dimly familiar faces, met at the whirl of his marriage. This intensely tight-knit family, living constantly in view of each other, resembles the extended-family systems of India. Its strength lies so much in the closeness of the members and their protectiveness towards each other. To leave this warm security must take an iron will and boundless ambition.

It is a few days later, after having met Alma's other brothers and sisters, one of whom has just given birth to a boy in the Memphis Naval Hospital, that I get the opportunity to meet Ike Lemmon.

He comes to Bernice's trailer house, chuckling over the small deception of having told his wife he'd just gone to visit some folk. He is shy and courteous and insists on calling this stranger "suh."

"I never did get to go to school much," Ike Lemmon says. "My father couldn't afford that. He needed me to drive the mule and chop cotton, so I quit schoolin' when I was very young. We didn't do no sharecroppin'. He had a little of his own land, sixty-seven acres to be exact, and we farmed it when we could and other times we worked for the white man. My father's name was Hal Lemmon and he didn't tell me much about what it was like in his days, 'cept it had been hard, hard times. His daddy was a slave, but he'd been sold away when he was young. He stops, sighs. "White people are sure hard to get on with. When they tell you to move on, you got to move on. Yassuh, white people have told me that and I've moved on. Better than the trouble they'll cause you.

"Things were cheap in those days. Snuff was twenty-five cents, and tobacco a nickel. We didn't get paid much either. A dollar a day for our work. A bell would ring at twelve so we could have lunch and then we'd keep workin' on til six in the evenin'.

"I met my wife at St. John's church and courted her four, five years before I married her. I was twenty-one years old then. It was sure a good thing my daddy had his own land, and he'd built his own house, 'cause otherwise we'd have had to live on white people's land, and that wouldn't have been so good. It was cheap to build your own house then . . . now it costs too much." This reminds him of something very different. "Yassuh, I did see a hangin' once, back in the '30s. They hung Tony Badge down by the church. I'm not sure of the exact story, but from what I heard they said he was goin' with another man's wife. I don't know whether that was true, 'cause I also heard that this white woman asked Tony to get her cotton in . . . that was from the number 9 field . . . and Tony didn't want to. She told him if he refused she'd have him killed. He begun to run away and she called after him that he'd never escape. 'I'm gonna have you killed,' she shouted. He did some runnin', but he didn't know where to hide. Ted Hall found him lyin' under the bed in his house, and Tony says to him, 'They're gonna kill me, I know.' Ted says, 'No they won't. They can't do that.' And he tol' him to hide somewhere else. They found Tony and put a rope on him and dragged him behind a car and then hung him down by the church. I saw that. Yassuh, we was all afraid. The white people could do that and there was nothin' we could do.

"The only time I've been out of Tennessee was when I joined the Army in '42. I went to Germany and Belgium and France. Yassuh, I saw some action, and it was nice seeing those countries and meetin' those people. When I come back, things began to change a bit. There's been lots

168

of changes now. Mostly things have gotten more expensive. In those days snuff was twenty-five cents, and tobacco a nickel."

Arthur only spends two days in Boston, crashing in Heywood's apartment. On his way back to Eufaula, he picks up Alma and Tavis from Memphis. His only report on Boston is that "it's gotten cold."

CHAPTER 13

Day By Day

On Monday, October 23, at 3:15 P.M., Arthur sets off
from home to start his new job at Roller Die. There is only
Alma and Tavis to see him off, as Bud has taken the
school bus on its round, and Odie is visiting town.

Arthur is dressed simply. He.wears an old pair of jeans,
strong leather work boots and an open neck shirt. He
looks faintly embarrassed. This is the first time I've seen
him in work clothes. Through all our time together, he
has been an immaculate dresser, but now, though his
clothes are neat and clean, he seems to feel that somehow
he has been reduced. Alma, once having said goodbye,
returns to sit on the porch in the rocker, with Tavis by her
side, and as we turn out of the gate onto the road, I can
see her receding slowly.

Since returning a few days ago from Memphis, Alma
has become quiet. The energy and enthusiasm she revealed in Boston, and in the company of her family in

Tennessee, has visibly begun to wane. She is given to long silences; and those sidelong mocking glances in which one can catch an occasional flicker of despair.

Following Arthur's example, she has been to the state unemployment office.

"I was talking to one of the ladies about employment," Alma says, "and she said that even after I go to that school, Sparks Technical College, the chances are that I would only get a job where they'd be payin' somethin' like two sixty-five even with my associate's degree, which I thought was really bad. Then she said I would probably get a raise in January of '79, because that's when the minimum wage is goin' up to two ninety. Then I went to the hospital in Eufaula to see whether I could get a job as a nurse's aide, but they tell me that there's no openings. And there aren't going to be for a very long time." She stares down at the floor boards, her head low, her face hidden. "Whoever heard of a hospital never wanting staff? There's always turnover. Since I've been back I've been doing a lot of thinking and I know it's going to take more than me and Arthur to try to change Eufaula. It's going to take all the black people to change Eufaula, the old and the young."

Her silence is long, restless. She is floundering in these rejections and doesn't quite know how to fight back. Her dignity and her independence rests on her ability to support herself, not picking cotton, but in a clean, air-conditioned office.

"I know I *have* to find a job, but I also want to go to school," she says. "But the school is only days so I've got to find a job at night to support us. I have until December before school starts, so hopefully I can get a full-time job till then."

I now turn to watch Alma get slowly smaller and smaller. The house, the sky, the vast space surrounding her are the walls and ceilings of her cell.

The drive into Eufaula has now become familiar. Arthur is pleased to have returned. The formality he had assumed in Memphis is only a memory now. He keeps the window open, and the music low, his head cocked listening to the hum of his car. He had a slight accident returning to Eufaula. A car in front of him on the highway threw something, and he swerved to avoid it, but it did catch his gas tank and part of his undercarriage, and he's a bit worried.

"It don't sound right," Arthur says. "I got to take it into the garage tomorrow."

The car turns smoothly onto Route 431. Lake Eufaula's perennial calm is broken by the faint lapping traces of a motorboat now drifting towards the center. A couple of white men cast their lines and settle back into their seats. Along the shore, there are the minute figures of other fishermen. The silence and the afternoon sun are calming.

"My father and mother went to see the man in the bank," Arthur says after a long silence. "He tells them the same thing about me havin' to make money, even though my father says he'll give the land and help on the payments." He shrugs as if trying to unsettle the load slowly descending on his shoulders. "And Alma's havin' trouble gettin' a job. She tol' you, Right? We thought it would be easy for her to get work here, but they say it's goin' to be awful hard. An' she sure don't want to work in no house or stuff like that. Even when she goes to school to get the proper education to get . . . a good job, they say she'll have to start at minimum wage. It's as if you haven't been to school at all. They told her all the factories around here have got their full quota. The idea has crossed my mind now if we made the right decision. Y'see, it depends so much on us gettin' this house together. If we . . . get it, things will work out for the better. At the present I don't know. It seems like every time we go to the bank, there's somethin' different that comes up. What do you think I should do?"

172

"Give it time."

"How long is . . . time?"

"Few months, I'd say."

We drive the rest of the way to Roller Die in silence. I am uneasily aware that the only panacea I can offer to his troubles is a bland cliché. Neither of us have the power to sway banking institutions or white employers.

In spite of the long, bright neons, the factory building is gloomy. Arthur reports to the foreman of the night shift. Pat Wilson is a short, square white man, and he perfunctorily gives Arthur a printed sheet of safety instructions, and then leads him to one of the machines. There are four rows of machines, which take up about a third of the factory space. Ribbons of steel of various widths are fed in at one end, shaped by a die, and then cut by another machine to the appropriate length. Arthur Dean's coworker on his machine is a white man, Jim. Jim is taciturn and merely nods his head to acknowledge Arthur's presence. The job is simple. All that Arthur and Jim have to do is lift the cut piece of metal off the machine and stack it in a neat pile. Once an hour the ribbon of steel runs out, and they have to replace it with a fresh one. At 8 P.M. they take a half-hour dinner break, so that the evening's work can end by 11:30.

The instructions take less than ten minutes and by 4:15 P.M. he is trapped by the machine's unending supply of precisely cut strips of steel. He lifts, he stacks, he lifts, he stacks, he lifts, he stacks. He glances up only once—and will not meet my eye.

The days grow short now. The sun's warmth does not extend into the shadows or the evenings. Its light seems to be so much sharper, and so clear that the trees and the house and the woods appear brittle. Sounds are still more muted, almost hurried, as if everything is aware that the nights will now come quicker, and remain longer. The nights are not cold as up in the North, but an overcoat is

173

needed to keep out this permanent chill. It touches the bones at times, and lies next to them, and one tries to remember what a summer was like.

Bud and Odie have long paced themselves to the moods of this land. They do not quicken the pace, but make the subtle adjustments necessary for the coming winter. On Friday, Bud takes three of his cows into the market in Doulton, and sells them for thirty-nine cents a pound.

"That's a good price," Bud says as we walk in the pasture behind the house. "They weighed 'round five hundred pounds each, so I guess I made some money on them. Had them since they was calves. That'll help pay for the winter feed for the others, and maybe by the spring I'll be able to sell a few more." He takes the cigar out of his mouth and surveys the remainder of his herd. There are thirty-seven head left and they amble slowly over towards him in the hope of feed. "I have to keep balancin' it: sell a few, buy a few. Can't afford to keep too many over the winter. I'll be sellin' off most of my hogs, they're costin' me too much."

Keith, as always, stumbles along, always within reach of Bud. He's become used to this stranger now, and no longer cries as much. He is as contented as I've ever seen him. Whatever the nightmare that haunts him, it has begun to recede.

Bud and Arthur are working on the pickup that has been parked under the pecan tree for so long. They've fixed a winch to one of the branches and have lifted the old engine out, and at the moment are fitting in the new one and making all the adjustments necessary to the gearbox and the crankshaft. Bud needs the pickup to haul his cattle to market and to carry feed. Renting one with a trailer is working out to be too expensive.

They work during the late morning and early afternoons, happy with each other's company. They are like old friends, each aware what the other should do, and

174

only occasionally stopping to discuss a particular technical problem. Arthur enjoys these sessions of work and he's quick to explain each technical move at length, as if to show he's capable of more than just lifting and stacking bits of metal off a machine.

"You're right," he says, peering under the chassis of the pickup. "It's very borin'. The guy Jim don't talk much, none of them do. Oh, he's okay. He's been workin' there five years." He shakes his head in wonder. "Some whites are real dumb. I wouldn't stay five years doin' that. Would you?"

"No."

"He keeps askin' me how much I'm makin'," Arthur says. "I think he's just tryin' to figure how much more than me he really makes. They always pay the white more for doin' the same job . . . I tol' you that didn't I? I overheard my foreman talkin' the other day with another white guy, and he sayin' that the rich whites really own this town, and all the rest of us, him included, got to do what they say. Could be true, but all whites speak with a forked tongue. When anythin' happens, they all stick together."

Odie calls for Bud to come to the house, and when Bud has left, Arthur works silently for a long time. Overhead a couple of fat squirrels peer down at the engine block.

"You know what I found out talkin' to the black guys at work?" Arthur said. "They don't want nothin'. They're happy just workin' one day to the next. The South really hasn't changed much you know. They got no goal in life, they just live for today. They're not strivin' for nothin'. That's the impression I get from the black people here. Just live from day to day, and what happen tomorrow just happen. They ain't got no plans, they don't know where they're goin'. You try and tell them to change, but they don't want to listen. They're scared."

Tavis wanders over from the house to watch his father

working for a while. He appears to be content here, and he and Keith seem to have reached a sort of truce. Tavis has decided to tolerate the foster boy, and now allows him on his tricycle and to accompany him on the short forays into the yard.

"There's a guy I met the other day," Arthur says. "He was workin' in Georgia, and 'cause his wife died he had to come on back to live here. Don't ask me why. Anyway, he's got four kids, and he's makin' somethin' like fifty dollars a week. I don' know how he lives. I just don't know. I couldn't do that. I want to give my family things, I sure don't want them to be eatin' one meal a day and runnin' round with no shoes. So I told the man he should go back to Georgia where he was makin' good money, but he don't listen. It's no good goin' on strike or stuff like that down here. They had a long strike last year at American Builders . . . that's the only international corporation here, and they pays the best money in town . . . but it didn't make no difference. They wouldn't give more money and just hired other blacks who wanted the work. It's goin' to be so difficult for us. More than I thought. I can't keep workin' at Roller Die for the kind of money they're payin'."

Bud returns to join Arthur on the pickup and for a while they talk quietly about the difficulties Arthur is having.

"I think you got to have a bit more patience," Bud tells Arthur. "Roller Die ain't much, but it's better than nothin'. When I was in town yesterday, I got to talkin' with the Chevy dealer, and he says that he could use you."

"Yeah? When?"

"In January, maybe."

"How much he payin?"

Bud pauses, and bites on his cigar. "He was talkin' somewhere round five, six dollars an hour. That's what you were makin' up in Massachusetts."

"Yeah!" Arthur considers that for a minute or two. "That ain't bad. Was he positive?"

"You go talk to him. I told him all about you, and he said he was sure interested. But not 'til the new year 'cause he won't have an openin' till then."

Arthur grunts. "I'll check him out tomorrow. If it's definite that he can hire me, then that'll be good news."

By early December, Odie has harvested her small crop of vegetables, and spent the days cooking and canning them. The glass jars gleam on the shelves, in the kitchen. Thanksgiving has been a particularly satisfying day for her. All her children, except for Arthur's brother in Boston, had gathered for the dinner. He had phoned earlier, promising to make the journey, but the day before he changed his mind. All the vegetables served at the dinner were hers, the chicken was from the yard, the ham from the hog killed a few days before. Only the turkey had been bought from the store. Odie had been happy to see Arthur Dean sit down with Denise and Agnes, and Bud and Alma and Tavis, and three foster girls and Keith.

Alma would have liked to have spent that Thanksgiving with her family in Memphis, but it couldn't be managed.

Alma's days have become too long, and the distances she travels each day too short. From the rear bedroom to the kitchen, too many hours in front of the television in the front bedroom. Her own bedroom appears to have shrunk. The suitcases are half-unpacked, clothes lie on the chair, the small closet is crammed to bursting. Her furniture lies in a warehouse in Eufaula. A couple of the pieces have been damaged in transit, and though Arthur has been almost daily to collect for the breakage, the white clerk has yet to examine his claims.

Alma shares the kitchen with Odie. Luckily, they have different times. Bud rises early, Arthur late. Bud eats at four in the evening, Arthur at midnight. It's been two months since she began to live in this house, and the kitchen still remains unfamiliar territory. She is getting dinner ready for Arthur, and trying to make as little sound as possible. Bud and Odie and the children have long gone to bed.

"The lifestyle I lead is so different from what I've been used to in the North," Alma sighs, heating up the cooking oil. "Like this . . . if this was my own home and own kitchen, I'd know where everything is and how everything's arranged and I don't have to go looking for this and looking for that. In my own home I'm the boss, I'm in charge. When we first left Boston, we had expectations that our house would be built in say, a couple of months. Now we just don't know anything. The bank says I've got to get a job, but where . . ."

She turns away, wiping her face. It is pleasantly warm in the kitchen, and once she has managed to discover Odie's hiding places for salt and pepper and other spices, she works quickly and efficiently.

"I even went to Doulton looking for a job," she continues. "It was in an electronics factory. The Man there said I could have one. It wasn't payin' much, like two thirty an hour, but it means travelin' a hundred and four miles every day. Fifty-two there, fifty-two back. Who's going to drive me? And even if I manage to get my own car, it's going to cost in gas."

She droops, and then makes an effort to stand straighter.

"Honestly, I'm tryin'," she says softly. "We can't even find an apartment in Eufaula. We've been looking everywhere. We went to Columbus too." She laughs derisively. "We had an appointment with this real estate agent, and we got there on time. We're just starting to discuss looking at houses, when this white couple walk in, and the real estate agent tells us to go for a walk and come back in half an hour. We left and never went back."

The night is quiet, except for the gentle hiss of cooking.

She can't play the radio too loud, and the only other sounds are the old house creaking, like an ancient ship rolling in the winds. The night outside is immense and dark. There are times it is so still, you can hear yourself breathe. "They're . . . they're now talking of building a home by themselves," Alma says. "Bud and Arthur. Oh God, can you imagine havin' a place exactly like this." She turns fierce. "I want a proper house, not this . . . collection of planks."

The days are spent watching soap operas. The gas fire is lit, and she sits close by, switching channels, flicking through *TV Guide*, searching desperately for something to hold her attention. Sometimes Odie joins her, or Keith or Tavis, at others the television set only lights her face alone.

"The worst part is wanting to be alone," Alma says. "I can't get to be alone here . . . there's always someone around. If I want to go into town to shop or even just for a ride, there's always someone who wants to come along with me. I just don't get a chance to be alone."

She has no friends in Eufaula. The only people she knows are the Stanfords and all the Stanford friends and relations. The only one that is near her age, and with whom she can sit and talk, is Denise. But Denise only comes home for the weekends. She is allowed to borrow her father's car, and on Saturdays, the two of them drive in Columbus or Phenix City to browse through the shops.

"I miss Boston, I miss my friends there, I miss the days I could get up and catch a bus and go downtown or do the different things I could do there that I can't do here," Alma says. "They don't have, like different shopping areas. They do but they're so far apart, like fifty or sixty miles apart. And whereas when I was in Boston, I could just catch a bus and go from one area to the next without any trouble. Because we have only one car and Arthur

Dean needs it, I have to stay at home. And if you don't have no car, you got to walk everywhere."

On a Friday night, for the lack of any alternatives, Alma and Denise and Agnes go to T.J.s. Arthur has to work every evening and Alma spends the hours watching her sisters-in-law dancing. Occasionally, she dances herself, but with little zest. In T.J.s the patrons are always the same, the music is always the same; only the disc jockeys differ.

"I've talked to blacks who live here," Alma says above the sound of the music. "And when you talk to them and tell them how far they're set back and that things need to change, they just look at you as if you're crazy. They say 'You can't change it, we've been like this all our lives, just 'cause you went away to Boston and Arthur went to Boston for seven years, don't mean we're goin' to change 'cause you've come back here. You have to do what we do.' But I'm not willing to do just they're doin'. The people here just live day to day and they just do what they have to do, they don't care—well I think they care—but they just feel there's nothing they can do to get the changes. They're not willing to try. I mean for jobs—they are so low paid and I think they should be getting more. But in order to get more, the people are going to have to get together, and they're scared. As long as they're getting enough to pay their bills, they don't need to be bothered with nobody else coming in tryin' to tell them what to do."

Denise, because of her youth and her ambitions, often becomes the focus of Alma's dissatisfaction with Eufaula.

"Sure, I'll go away," Denise interrupts, "but I'll always come back here. I love Eufaula, and I think you're exaggeratin'."

"That's 'cause you don't know no different. Once you go away, you'll see how things have changed everywhere else but here."

"Things are changin' here," Denise insists. "I'll always return here, and buy myself a big white house."

"Huh, they won't let you live on the same street as them," Alma says.

"I'll be a star then," Denise giggles, and vamps. "They won't have no chance to say no."

"Huh," Alma snorts, giving Denise a withering glance. "That won't make no difference. If I stayed here that's the only lifestyle I would want to live in, like these whites. I've been poor for a long time. I'm not saying I'm rich now, but I know how it is to live better. And the only people I see who're living real good here is the white people. When you arrive in Eufaula you see all the big mansions and stuff, then you look on the other side and see all the little shabby houses that are owned by black people. Then you say 'What's going on here.' The only people that's really getting anywhere is the white people. And you ask yourself why. Do you think that the black people just shut their eyes to what's happening here or they just don't care?"

"It's no good gettin' angry," Denise starts to say.

"Why not? What else is there for me to do?"

Saturdays drift in softly, unnoticed. It is no different than any other day, as it was in the city. Arthur wakes late and Alma makes his breakfast. He sits out on the porch in one of the rocking chairs, chewing toast, sipping coffee.

He takes Alma shopping and they're back by noon. Odie and Bud too have gone into town to buy Christmas presents for all the children. Denise is padding around the house in her nightgown.

On his return from shopping Arthur decides to take Tavis out shooting. He takes his .22 rifle and a pocket full of bullets, and with Tavis holding his hand, he wanders

181

off into the stand of trees. Alma refuses to accompany him.

"The only thing to do in Eufaula is to go to a movie," Alma says. "And there's only one movie house . . . and that's showin' soft porn. I can't take Tavis anywhere, can I?"

The highlight for the day is to be the football game between Eufaula High and Clayton High. Alma is totally uninterested in football, but Denise, who is familiar with all the local heroes, persuades her to accompany her to the game.

Arthur and Tavis return proudly with a dead squirrel. It has been riddled with bullets, and Arthur Dean relates in gory detail how he hit and missed.

"That's disgusting," Alma says.

"That's adventure," Arthur says, and carefully lays the squirrel down on the porch.

Even though it is still early afternoon, and the sun is bright, it has turned cold. Alma lights the gas fire in the front bedroom and switches on the television.

"I went and saw the Chevy dealer in Eufaula," Arthur says as he settles down on the floor in front of the fire. "He says . . . maybe he'll hire me in January. But maybe he won't. And Roller Die is . . ." He slumps down. "I thought I'd be doin' forty-eight hours a week, which would have helped with bills, but last week I only worked twenty. I go in every day, but if there's no work, they send me home and I don't get paid. A couple of days I even swept the floor, so's I could have the money." The fire crackles and glows and appears to mesmerize Arthur. "You know, I'm beginnin' to think I made a mistake."

Silence settles in the room. Arthur gropes for words, finds none, lapses back onto the floor. A cloud drifts across the sun, stealing light, and the room becomes a contrast between the gray of the television and soft yellow of the fire.

"What do you think I should do?" Arthur appeals to me.

It is an impossible question to answer. He is in anguish. He had saved for a year, and thought he'd prepared the family for the move, and now the earth has shifted, and he's falling.

"I think maybe give it till January. See what the Chevy dealer says."

"Yeah," he says, and looks at Alma. She doesn't meet his eye but stares at the television. "I am bein' patient, but you can also spend a lifetime waitin', you know. We were financially prepared, but I don't think we was prepared for what stood in our paths, you know. I mean our confidence in the things that we'd set out to do. We wasn't prepared enough in that respect. I knew the job wasn't goin' to pay as much as I made up in Boston, and I expected to take a drop of about a third. But two-thirds is ridiculous. And I didn't expect so many obstacles to stand in our pathway, you know. Maybe our expectations are too . . . too farfetched. Even just talkin' to people about what your plans are they say that, they think you're crazy or somethin' like that. I can't be content with what I can get here. My dreams are what I want, and I don't think I can accomplish them here."

"You're stammering more," Alma says, not unkindly.

"Yeah," and Arthur takes a breath. "I always do that when I get under pressure. It was worse in school. This teacher would deliberately make me stand up and talk, and laugh when I begun to stammer."

"I never knew that," Alma says. "I would have hit her if I'd been there."

"Then in the eighth grade," Arthur continues, "another teacher tol' me if I put a pebble under my tongue, I could stop stammerin'. I put a quarter, and it helped a while."

"I'm glad I never had that kind a problem," Alma says.

183

"But when I got to Boston, I was determined to speak properly. You know, without a Tennessee accent. It took me a year, and now I don't have one, do I?"

"No."

"I can never get rid of my accent," Arthur says. "I speak too slow for me to change to Northern."

At 3:45 in the afternoon, sticking to his routine, Arthur goes off to work. An hour or so later, Alma and Denise, with Denise driving her father's car, go to the football game in Eufaula.

It is an important event. For the first time in many years, Eufaula High has made the finals of the Alabama state high school championships. Most of the town and the community are at the stadium, and by the time we arrive the bands have started playing. The stands on either side of the football ground are filled with the white spectators, with a sprinkling of black faces; those behind the goal posts are filled with the black. There are no white faces among them. It is Alma's first football game, and unfortunately it is bitterly cold. She shivers in the stand and watches, with waning interest, the antics of the cheerleaders.

"I used to cheer for the basketball team in Baker Hill High," Denise says. "And I got to be the leader in the final year."

Alma remains mute while Denise chatters on about her high school days. Obviously, she had an enjoyable time. She is pretty enough to have been very popular.

"I never got to do that," Alma finally says softly. "We was too poor, and I had to go home and work."

Around us are exuberant black teenagers conducting their own cheering, and they are far more entertaining and far more talented than any of those dancing out on the field. The drizzle that has begun and the increasing cold fail to dampen their enthusiasm or their inventiveness.

"And this is what they call the big night in Eufaula,"

184

Alma says with sarcasm which isn't heard by the others.

We leave at the end of the third quarter with Eufaula High, led by a slight young black quarterback, leading thirty-five to eight.

Odie and Bud are near tears. Bud sits out on the porch in the rocker, the cigar still in his mouth, staring out at the sky. Odie sniffles and shuffles around the house, trying hard not to cry. A couple of hours ago, Keith's mother came and took him away from them.

"She phoned to say she was comin' to take Keith for a few days, and bring him back Sunday. Then she came and said she was goin' to keep him . . ." Odie dabs at her eyes, the glasses catch the glare of the room light. "I told her I'd bought him his Christmas presents—a little car and a new shirt—and she said 'Never mind, I'll get him some more.' Then she left. At the time I couldn't think of one question to ask, now I have a thousand. I won't have him back, unless he stays and is old enough to decide for himself. Not otherwise. It's bad for him, and bad for me." She sits back. Age suddenly appears to have raced ahead of her, and caught her by surprise. "I don't know what to do with his presents."

It takes a while for Bud to talk about Keith. He avoids the subject for some time and then blurts out: "I miss him somethin' terrible. An' I know he misses me. He ain't gone too far . . . just up the road. I sometimes think of visitin' him, but it wouldn't be good for either of us." He sighs heavily. "The place seems empty without him."

As Christmas draws nearer, Bud and Odie sense the disquiet in their son. He appears quieter to them and is given to walking slowly around the front yard, head bent, kicking at his precious dust. They have spoken and listened, and know another emptiness is about to enter their household.

"We're movin' on," Oddie tells Arthur Dean one

evening as they sit in front of the fire. "You're the ones that are stayin'. Someone's got to look after all this we have. You leave it and people will come and take it away. But I can't tell you what you should do."

Bud lights his cigar for the first time in a couple of days and takes a couple of puffs. The smoke is whisked away in the strong breeze. He lets the cigar die and chews on it.

"I will be very sad if he goes back North," he says. "But I ain't askin' too many questions."

CHAPTER 14

The Defeat

I can feel Arthur's pain. He keeps asking me what I would do if I were him, and it is an impossible question for me to answer. All that I can do is to question him, in the hope that his thoughts will become clearer for himself.

"Where do you really want to live, Arthur?"

"Here, near my family. I really don't want to return North ever."

"Then why don't you remain here?"

"I'm not makin' the money," Arthur says, as we stroll around his yard. We seem to move in ever decreasing circles, kicking at the dust. "I've got to make the kind of money I made in Boston. Besides, Alma . . ." And he trails off.

Alma is clearly very unhappy. She either watches television all day or else sits in the rocker on the porch staring mutely out at the horizon. She has given up all hope of getting a job, and also made the deicision that she wants to return North to Boston.

"What would you do if you was me?" Arthur asks me once more. The litany of questions and answers has been going on for days, and I ask him once more what he really wants to do. Alma, who has been sitting in the rocker, glancing occasionally at us, joins us.

"I've told you what I want to do," she tells Arthur. "I want to go back to Boston. If you want to stay, you can stay. But I'm going."

"I think we should give it time," Arthur pleads.

"Time!" Alma glances scornfully at both of us. "I got no more time. I told you, you can stay if you want. I've had enough of this place. I'll take Tavis and go back to Boston."

A silence settles between them. Uneasy, hard. They won't look at each other. Alma holds herself, and shivers. Though the sun is out, throwing sharp shadows across their faces, the wind is strong and cruel. It hurries the dust, and snaps at Alma's hair.

"He's happy here," Alma turns to me. "He works on that car all morning with his father, and then goes off to work. What the hell do I do?"

"I like workin' with my father on the car," Arthur says defensively. "We got it runnin' yesterday. Not far, but it ran. Just a few more things . . ."

"I'm goin'," Alma cuts him short. It's more a challenge than a statement. "I told you, I'm not going to be poor all my life. That's what's gonna happen if we stay on here."

Arthur nods mutely. "I'm just not makin' enough money to pay our bills. I don't know how people live. I met this guy an' he had a good job in Georgia, but 'cause his wife died he came back to live here. He's making maybe fifty, sixty dollars a week, and he's got four kids. I don't know how he does it. I couldn't."

"That's 'cause he doesn't want nothing," Alma says in disgust. "He's quite happy eating one meal a day. I'm not going to be like that."

"I'm goin' to wait till Christmas," Arthur suddenly says decisively. "I should be gettin' a bonus from the company and that'll help us."

"You don't think they're going to give you a bonus, do you?" Alma asks in disbelief.

"They might," Arthur says, and before Alma can interrupt he continues. "If you work there ninety days, they say they give you a bonus. One of the guys there was expectin' a turkey as his bonus on Thanksgivin' day. He'd have been there eighty-nine days. So he asks them if he's gonna get a turkey, and they tell him 'yes.' So he don't buy no turkey, and on the night before Thanksgivin' when they're givin' out turkey, they don't give him one. They tell him he's only worked eighty-nine days. So then he phones his wife, and tells her to get a turkey, but they ain't any left."

"That was mean of the company," Alma says. "If I was that guy I'd have punched the boss in the mouth."

"He didn't do nothin'. I'd have got real mad and quit. But he's still workin' there." Arthur pauses a moment. "I don't suppose they'll give me anythin' either."

"I don't know whether I'm going to stay around till Christmas," Alma says. "I could be back in Boston tomorrow and have a job the day after. Then I'll have some spending money for Christmas." She studies Arthur a long while. "I'm going."

Arthur and I watch her march back into the house. We still watch when the door slams shut, as if we are expecting her to come out with her bags packed. Arthur turns away finally and looks out over his land.

"We'll never get the money to build that house," he says sadly. "We just can't save it workin' here."

We slowly follow Alma back into the house.

A few days before Christmas, Arthur quits his job at Roller Die. They pack the car with their clothes and start off back to Boston. But then, Arthur changes his mind. He wants to spend Christmas with his family. As Alma also wants to spend Christmas with hers, he drives her to Memphis and returns to Eufaula alone to be with Bud and Odie and Denise and Agnes.

CHAPTER 15

Boston

Mascot Street in Dorchester, Massachusetts, isn't far from Evelyn Street in Mattapan. Not more than a quarter of a mile separates the two, but the distance traveled is more like a couple of thousand. The streets are similar. The houses on Mascot Street, as on Evelyn, are two- and three-story apartment buildings: wood-framed, with sloping porches and triangular shingled roofs. The children playing on the sidewalk are black, and here and there, are the beginnings of abandonments. Empty houses with broken windows, tracts of razed land, a few junked cars. In early January, the trees that should be shading the small, ragged lawns and the sidewalks are as bare and dark as the sides of these weatherworn houses.

Arthur and Alma are lucky. One of Alma's friends had heard of an apartment falling vacant, and as soon as she knew Alma was returning, she'd reserved it for them. They couldn't move in immediately, as they neither had the money nor the jobs to support themselves. Instead, when they arrived in Boston on January 10th, having driven up from Eufaula via Memphis, they stayed with Alma's sister Doc.

It takes Alma all of three days to find herself a job. It is with American Mutual as a filing clerk.

"I'm so happy to be back here," Alma says. "I was going mad down in Eufaula doing nothing all day. Look how easy it is here to get work, and that's all I wanted. Now I'm gonna go to night school and get myself a business diploma."

The transformation in Alma is quite visible, almost tangible. She laughs easier, and she is full of that old energy. The apartment they found is bigger than the old one, and the moment all their furniture comes up from the warehouse in Eufaula, they move in. The apartment is on the ground floor and has two bedrooms, a living room and a dining room. Alma decides she doesn't need a dining room and extends the living room into the dining room. Tavis's bedroom is decorated with Spiderman curtains and Spiderman sheets and pillow cases.

Alma enrolls in the Burdett Business School to study, two evenings a week, shorthand, typing, filing and charm. Charm?

"Yeah," Alma laughs. "They teach you how to please your boss. You know, how to adjust to his personality, what to wear to work, what men like."

Arthur is quieter than his usual self. He also had little difficulty finding work at a wage he could accept without a loss of dignity. It is with the Dupont Company as a warehouseman. He is enrolling in Northeastern Technical College to study industrial electronics.

"I keep thinkin' that I didn't do somethin' right," Arthur says, sitting in his living room. "I thought I was really prepared but . . ." He blinks rapidly, staring at the walls. "I learned one thing. You got to have a qualification if you want to move South and earn the same money. If you're like us—ordinary people—you don't have much of a chance. I don't like Boston. One day, I'm goin' back, goin' home, for good."